MW01107634

JOHN
tells the
TRUTH

Bryan Norford

Pebble Press

John tells the Truth

Copyright © 2017 Bryan Norford

ISBN-10: 1973907356
ISBN-13: 978-1973907350

All rights reserved. No part of this publication may be reproduced, stored in a retrieval system, or transmitted in any form, or by any means—electronic, mechanical, photocopy, recording, or any other—except for brief quotations in printed reviews, without prior permission.

All Scripture references are taken from the HOLY BIBLE, NEW INTERNATIONAL VERSION copyright © 1973, 1978, 1984 by the International Bible Society, copyright by Zondervan © 2005. Used by permission of Zondervan Publishing House. All rights reserved.

Cover photo from Pixabay:
Typical scenery where the Dead Sea scrolls were found in 1947.

Dedication

To our latest great grandsons:
Ezra Matthew Yuydzen Horch and Jesse Lee Alexander.
God grant that they will grow up to know the truth.
and freely express it throughout their lives

.

Books by Ann and Bryan Norford

Happy Together: Daily Insight for Families from Scripture
War Kids: Growing Up in World War Two England

Books by Bryan Norford

Guess Who's Coming to Reign: Jesus Talks about His Return
Gone with the Spirit: Tracking the Holy Spirit through the
    Bible
Jesus: Is He Really God? Does It Really Matter?
Anointed Preaching: The Holy Spirit and the Pulpit
Getting to Know You 1: Seeking God in the Old Testament
Getting to Know You 2: Finding Christ in the New Testament
Prostate Cancer: My Story of Survival
The Silent Remainder, a Novel
The Little book on Revelation

"For this reason I was born,
and for this I came into the world,
to testify to the truth.
Everyone on the side of truth listens to
me."

John 18:37

Contents

Appendices

Introduction

John's Distinctive Gospel

The four gospels, Matthew, Mark, Luke, and John are the only detailed record we have of the life, death, and resurrection of Jesus. We cannot know Him without a study of these gospels. However, John's gospel is distinctive. Matthew, Mark, and Luke (called the synoptic gospels) are mostly narrative, written thirty to forty years earlier than John's gospel. While this study concentrates on John, we will include material from the other gospels where it is helpful.

John, with time and hindsight, adds theological understanding to his writings. Like the evangelists, John wrote his gospel in Greek, the international language of the day. It was a well-developed philosophical language ideal for transmission of thought, and many of the world's classical writings emerged in this language.

But these factors do not make John's gospel more difficult to understand. John, an unschooled fisherman, used a distinctive form of the Greek language, known as Koiné Greek, the language of the common man. John is a good starting point to learn New Testament Greek because it is the simplest Greek in the New Testament, one a child could read. Yet John's gospel contains some of the most sublime truths of Scripture.

John concentrates his message on the deity of Jesus Christ. He makes direct declarations in his prologue, 1:1–18, and records Jesus Christ's direct claims, notably 4:26, 8:58, 13:14, and 18:37. Furthermore, Jesus constantly refers to His origin from above. Note especially His saying "I have come down from heaven" six times in chapter 6. Similar references, such as "from above," and "from the Father," are liberally sprinkled throughout John's gospel. But Jesus uses two other, much clearer ways of ensuring the Jews understood exactly what He was declaring.

First, John is unique in repeating Jesus' use of the emphatic "*I am*" statements throughout his gospel. Jesus does this by doubling the pronoun "I" in these statements, clear in Greek, but not easily translated into English. We have italicized these emphatic uses of "*I am*" throughout the chapters of this book to alert you to its use. This doubling of the personal pronoun "I" compares to the Hebrew idiom God uses about Himself, specifically found in Isaiah 43:11 and 25, 48:15 and 51:12.

That would have been enough to raise the disquiet of His Jewish listeners. But Jesus bluntly uses it in John 8:58 to claim God's name from Exodus 3:13–14, for which the Jews tried to stone Him for perceived blasphemy. See Appendix A for a list and explanation of the "I am" sayings of Jesus recorded by John.

Second, Jesus refers to Himself as the "Son of Man" over eighty times in the four gospels and over thirty times in John's gospel. While we might regard this saying as referring to His humanity, in fact, the Jews would understand a different and specific meaning from the Old Testament.

The Son of Man was the Messiah the Jews were expecting. Daniel 7:13–14 describes Him: a Son of Man brought before the "Ancient of Days" and given "authority, glory and sovereign power; all peoples, nations and men of every language worshiped Him. His dominion is an everlasting dominion that will not pass away, and His kingdom is one that will never be destroyed." See Appendix B for a fuller explanation how Jesus' use of this title contributed to His crucifixion and will herald His return to earth.

John's gospel is also sparse with his record of Jesus' miracles. He is more concerned with the meaning than the marvel of the miracles. John chooses each to specifically highlight a facet of Jesus' deity, and in doing so calls the miracles he records "signs." See a list of John's recorded miracles and their potential meaning in Appendix C.

John's Passion for the Truth

John's work emphasizing the deity of Christ and the truth of His claims was not just an academic exercise. He had a specific outcome in mind. John wrote these things so "you may believe that Jesus is the Christ, the Son of God, and that by believing you may have life in His name," 20:31.

However, for belief to be effective it must be based on what is true and real. That is why John concentrates on the truth of what he records about Jesus. Popular ideas of personal truth through intuition, or communal truth by democratic consensus, must eventually collapse, built on the shifting sands of "relative" truth.

The Deity of Jesus Christ is John's basis for all truth throughout his gospel. The reason "heaven and earth will pass away, but my words will never pass away," Matthew 24:35, is because Jesus' words conform to the ultimate reality of all God is and has created. The writer to the Hebrews says Jesus is "The exact representation of God's being," and "through whom He made the universe," he also added, "In these last days [God] has spoken to us by His Son," Hebrews 1:1–3.

Jesus was "full of grace and truth," and claimed, "I *am* the truth." Not only did Jesus make truth claims, He declared Himself the embodiment of truth. Contrary to popular western opinion, Jesus is the source of the absolute truth that encompasses all of life. All other truth claims are a false foundation for life. So John uses the word "truth" over fifty times in his gospel.

The corollary of truth is to believe, and John uses this verb eighty-five times. But for belief to be secure and effective, it must be in an objective truth that transcends mere personal and public opinion. John claims Jesus Christ is the sole source of this truth.

3

As if to emphasize the concern for truth, all four gospel writers use the phrase, "I tell you the truth," with which Jesus prefaced certain critical truths He wished to stress. In John's gospel, the King James Version (KJV) of the Bible translated word for word, "Verily, verily [or truly, truly] I say unto you." John records Jesus' use of this phrase twenty-six times.

The force of this in the original is equivalent to saying: "Listen carefully and retain this important, critical truth I am about to tell you." Of course, whatever Jesus spoke was truth, but the bland, "I tell you the truth," in modern translations misses the critical nature of some overriding truths Jesus wished to impart. In the notes for each chapter, where these occur they are labeled as a critical truth. In each case, the quotation is repeated in full, inset and italicized for clearer prominence. Appendix D lists these sayings.

Therefore, this study of John will focus on John's concern for believing in Jesus' claims of truth. While notes on each passage will provide explanation for the general text of John's gospel, they will highlight statements regarding truth, which will deepen the certainty of your faith.

The question is often raised whether the gospel accounts are reliable, especially the accounts of the resurrection. If they are not reliable, they are not true, and Christ's claims are false. Appendix E sets out factors authenticating the gospel accounts.

Some Explanatory Notes.

Do not be confused between the two Johns of the gospels. John A, the Apostle is the one writing this gospel, but he refers throughout his gospel to John B, the Baptist. In the first chapter, John A refers to John B in verses 6–8, as the forerunner, or presenter of Jesus Christ. John B was not one of the disciples and Herod beheaded him during Jesus' three years ministry.

Chapter numbers in this book repeat the chapter numbers in John. Each chapter has a brief introduction, followed by groups of verses providing explanatory comments. Bible references include the book name unless they refer to a text in John, where we omit the book name. There is no reference if the quotation is from the text range under review. Quotations are from the New International Version (NIV) of the Bible.

You will find several appendices at the latter part of the book, generally referenced from this introduction or chapters relevant to the subject of each.

Major Divisions

Prologue: 1:1–18. Establishes Jesus' identity and the need of faith.

Public Ministry: 1:19 to 12:50. Jesus' proclamation of truth and its acceptance or rejection by the Jews.

Ministry to His Disciples: chapters 13:1 to 17:26. Prepares them for His death and departure, and their future ministry.

Crucifixion and Resurrection: chapters 18:1 to 21:23. John's eyewitness account.

Epilogue: chapter 21:24–25. Final purpose and instructions.

1

John the Baptist Introduces Jesus Christ

"Look, the Lamb of God,
who takes away the sin of the world!"

John 1:29

The first part of the first chapter of John's gospel, verses 1–18, introduces the person of Jesus Christ. John clearly identifies Jesus Christ as God, the divine person of the Trinity descended to earth to take away the sin of the world. Throughout the remainder of his gospel, John continues to reveal the deity of Christ.

The remainder of the first chapter of John divides easily into two sections. In the opening section, John presents Jesus Christ as He begins His ministry, verses 19–34. In the final section, John records Jesus selecting His first disciples as He prepares to launch His ministry, verses 35–51. These two sections document the first few days of Jesus' ministry.

John Identifies Jesus Christ

1-3   John has no hesitation in asserting the deity of Christ in his first words. Note his repeat of the first words of the Old Testament, Genesis 1:1, "In the beginning."

Beginning of what? Creation? Eternity?

"Beginning" is a time word, part of creation. Jesus, the Word, was there before the beginning of time, compare 17:5 and Colossians 1:17. The other gospel writers commence their stories at the ministry of Jesus, (Mark) or with birth and lineages back to Abraham (Matthew) or Adam (Luke). John reaches back to creation and before, pointing out that Jesus was a co-creator of the universe, along with the other members of the Trinity, God the Father and the Holy Spirit, Genesis 1:1–2.

Note the attributes John gives to Jesus:

"The Word was with God," a *separate person* from God the Father.

"And the Word was God," *equal* in essence and substance with the Father.

"He [the Word] was with God in the beginning," *eternal* as God.

John emphasizes the role of Jesus at creation: "Through Him all things were made; without Him nothing was made that has been made." As all three members of the Trinity were active at creation, it is reasonable to expect they left their mark on creation.

Indeed they have. Three elements form all of creation: Space, Matter and Time. Each has three components. Space: height, length, and width; Matter: solid, liquid, and gas; Time: past, present, and future. But the Trinity is supremely represented in the family: father, mother, and child—one or more. Recall God's mandate to create humanity: "Let *us* make man in *our* own image, in *our* likeness," Genesis 1:26, my emphasis.

In these first three verses of John's gospel, John calls Jesus "the Word," from the Greek "<u>Logos</u>." For the Greeks, Logos meant the rational principle that governs all things. John presents the Person of Jesus Christ as the governing principle of all things. Paul, and the writer of Hebrews, both declare Jesus as Creator and Sustainer of all things, Colossians 1:15–17 and Hebrews 1:1–3.

All this denies us the paternalistic nonsense that Jesus was just a good man. The Bible, especially John's emphatic disclosure of the identity of Jesus Christ, does not give us that option.

4–5   John singles out two characteristics of Jesus in these verses: life and light. In his gospel, John continually points to Jesus as the source of life. Without Him, life cannot exist; it will wither and die. Then, John declares Jesus' life is the basis of "the light of men."

Now natural light by which we see is certainly a part of God's creation: "And God said, 'Let there be light,' and there was light," Genesis 1:3. The sun, moon, and stars separated the night from the day providing light, and confirmed the creation of natural light necessary for us to live and survive.

God is light. Natural light only exists where He is. He created light before He created the sun three days later. He, God the Father, and the Lamb the Son, are the light of heaven—no sun or moon is necessary, Revelation 21:22 and 22:5. That is why hell is complete darkness, for God is absent. He honours the choice of those who reject Him.

But for John, as with much of Scripture, light is also a metaphor for truth and understanding, for life is only possible where truth exists and is upheld. Compare Isaiah 9:2, "The people walking in darkness have seen a great light; on those living in the land of the shadow of death a light has dawned." John proclaims darkness has failed against the light of truth: "the darkness has not understood [or overcome] it."

The root of the Greek verb used here is to seize. John states the darkness has failed to defeat, conquer, commandeer, or triumph, over the truth. Darkness is the absence of truth. Paul elaborates. Those who suppress and discard the truth descend into futile thinking and darkened minds, Romans 1:18–21. As long as humans seek to supplant the truth with their own deficient reasoning, the world will increasingly descend into darkness and ensuing chaos, "For the foolishness of God is wiser than man's wisdom," 1 Corinthians 1:25.

This separation of truth and falsehood, light and darkness, is the basis of Jesus' determination to proclaim the truth. "I *am* the light of the world. Whoever follows me will never walk in darkness, but will have the light of life," 8:12, and, "For this reason I was born, and for this I came into the world, to testify to the truth. Everyone on the side of truth listens to me," 18:37.

9–13   This true light that lights the life of all men came into the world. He became flesh and blood like us, leaving behind His power and glory to share in our weakness and pain, and ultimately to be crucified for us in our place. Philippians 2:6–8, referring to Jesus proclaims, "Who, being in very nature God, did not consider equality with God something to be grasped, but made Himself nothing, taking the very nature of a servant, being made in human likeness. And being found in appearance as a man, He humbled Himself and became obedient to death–even death on a cross!"

His coming was at great personal price. Those He created, who were His own, and whom He loved, rejected Him. They did not recognize Him. John's gospel repeatedly recounts those who heard His words always divided into those who believed Him and those who did not. Jesus highlighted the original and ongoing conflict between believers and non-believers.

Jesus foretold the majority would reject Him, "Enter through the narrow gate. For wide is the gate and broad is the road that leads to destruction, and many enter through it. But small is the gate and narrow the road that leads to life and only a few find it," Matthew 7:13–14. That most people disbelieve, does not invalidate those who believe in Jesus Christ.

John broadcast the good news, the Gospel. Those who believe in Jesus and receive Him as the light and life for their lives become children of God, not born by natural means but "born of God." Recall Jesus' message to Nicodemus, 3:7: "You must be born again."

Paul declares the glorious destiny of those who believe: "Flesh and blood cannot inherit the Kingdom of God, nor does the perishable inherit the imperishable. Listen, I tell you a mystery: We will not all sleep, but we will all be changed—in a flash, in the twinkling of an eye, at the last trumpet. For the trumpet will sound, the dead will be raised imperishable, and we will be changed," 1 Corinthians 15:50–52.

14–18   John says, "we have seen His glory, the glory of the one and only (or only begotten)." In his first letter, John confirms Jesus is the one "which we have heard, which we have seen with our eyes, which we have looked at and our hands have touched—this we proclaim concerning the Word of life," 1 John 1:1–2.

In verses 14 and 17, John twice talks of grace and truth coming through Jesus Christ. "The law was given through Moses; but grace and truth came through Jesus Christ." The Law is good, Paul says, Romans 7:12–13, but it cannot save, only convict. Paul adds in Romans 5:20, "The law was added so that the trespass might increase."

However, Paul goes on to explain, "Where sin increased, grace increased all the more, so that, just as sin reigned in death, so also grace might reign through righteousness to bring eternal life through Jesus Christ our Lord," Romans 5:20-21. The grace of Jesus Christ can provide us with forgiveness and reconciliation with God. Thus John says, "From the fullness of His grace we have all received one blessing after another." His grace comes in waves for every situation of life.

But what is grace? Commonly defined as "unmerited favour," that definition better fits mercy. Grace includes empowerment. When Paul complained about his "thorn in the flesh," God said to him, "My grace is sufficient for you, for my power is made perfect in weakness," 2 Corinthians 12:9. And as John says, "we receive the right [or authority, or empowerment] to become children of God." Grace is more than mercy and forgiveness, it provides power for living, better defined as "God's empowering presence."

Alongside grace, the basis of our reconciliation with God, is John's first mention of truth coming and found in Christ, a foremost thrust of his gospel. If Jesus Christ is not the basis of all truth, all the gospels and the New Testament tell us about the promised life here and hereafter is nonsense. Christ is the basis for all things, not only as Creator, but also Sustainer of all things. Without Him, all that exists would cease to be, leaving only the blackness of the uncreated.

Jesus came as the fundamental, authoritative, universal, and absolute truth of life. He is the Truth, 14:6. Either we believe Him and in Him, or we make up our own "truth." Current common wisdom declares truth is always relative—we all carry our own truth, no longer defined by reason, but by our subjective intuition, which can never be a substitute for Christ's objective and constant truth worthy of our faith.

Find God in the person of Jesus Christ. Jesus has made God known, verse 18. In fact, Jesus is the earthly personification of God: "Don't you know me, Philip, even after I have been among you such a long time? Anyone who has seen me has seen the Father," 14:9. The writer to the Hebrews describes Him this way: "The Son is the radiance of God's glory and the exact representation of His being, Hebrews 1:3.

Men once believed that the sun revolved around the earth, understandable from simple observation. But space flight would not have been possible without the correct understanding how the planets, including our own, revolve around the sun. Similarly, only an accurate understanding of the facts of life: God, in Christ, as Creator of the cosmos, Giver and Sustainer of life, and Redeemer of humanity from sin, will provide us with a truthful and sustainable understanding of life, here and for eternity.

We no longer need to live in the doldrums of existence dispensed by the lies of the evil one, 10:10. Jesus came to bring life in its fullness. His grace and truth are the basis of life.

John the Baptist Witnesses to Jesus Christ

19–23   John the Baptist (John B) was baptizing Jews. Normally, the Jews considered only Gentiles needed cleansing, but John was calling the nation of Israel to repentance, especially the Jewish leadership. His message of judgment and repentance for Israel echoed that of Elijah. Hear John's uncompromising message: "You brood of vipers ! Who warned you to flee from the coming wrath?" Matthew 3:7. Furthermore, he must have appeared as the Jews would remember Elijah, "A man with a garment of hair and with a leather belt around his waist," 2 Kings 1:8.

The Jewish delegation, priests, Levites and Pharisees, responsible for politically correct theology, questioned John's authority. John emphatically denied he was the Christ, or Messiah. The Jews would recall Elijah did not die, 2 Kings 2:11. Was this Elijah returned to earth? Elijah was certainly expected back, Malachi 4:5, and John came in the "spirit and power of Elijah," Luke 1:13–17. Compare Jesus' words, Matthew 17:11–12, where Jesus claimed John the Baptist was Elijah, certainly in influence if not in person. According to the Passover enactment, the Jews are still expecting Elijah to return.

Perhaps John was the prophet predicted in Deuteronomy 18:15 and 18, whom Peter recognized as Jesus, Acts 3:22. In all these suggestions John was adamant he was not, "No!" Exhausting the possibilities, they asked who he was. John quoted Isaiah 40:3: "A voice of one calling: 'In the desert prepare the way for the Lord; make straight in the wilderness a highway for our God.'"

24–28   The Pharisees considered John the Baptist illegitimate if he was not one of the above, and should not be baptizing. John answered he baptized with water as a forerunner of Jesus the Messiah, who was already among them, and who would baptize with the Holy Spirit, verse 33.

He is the One they "do not know." Throughout the gospel, the Jewish leadership refused to recognize Him, recall 1:11. However, John recognized Him so far superior to himself; he could not stoop to do the most menial task, that of unlatching His sandals.

29–34   John was baptizing at Bethany, not the one close to Jerusalem where Mary and Martha lived. It's unknown location "on the other side of the Jordan," was certainly on the Jordan river as water was there for baptism.

Note the sequence of following days, here and in the remainder of the chapter. "The next day," John fulfilled his mandate, pointing to Jesus, "the Lamb of God who takes away the sin of the world." Christ can cover every sin committed throughout earth's history, sufficient for all, but only effective for those will believe. Compare Isaiah 53:6, and 1 John 2:1–2. Only the blood of Jesus can cleanse from sin, Jews and Gentiles alike.

John noted that Jesus "was before me," although Jesus was born six months after John. John recognized Jesus' pre-existence before His earthly birth, so recognizing Jesus' greater majesty and place before John–from before the world began, 1 Peter 1:18–20, Revelation 13:8.

John claimed he did not know Jesus, although he and Jesus were relatives born six months apart. More likely, John did not necessarily know Him as the Christ, and waited for a sign to identify Him. The sign was the Spirit coming and resting on Him, fulfilled at Jesus' baptism, Compare Isaiah 11:1–2. That sign was fulfilled as John baptized Jesus, see Matthew 3:13–17. Subsequently, John testified to, and identified Jesus as, the "Son of God."

Jesus Selects His First Disciples.

35–39   The following day, John again pointed out "the Lamb of God" to two of his disciples. This was probably deliberate, a "passing on" of his disciples and fame to Christ.

Recall John the Baptist's later assertion, "He must become greater; I must become less," 3:30.

On hearing that, the two disciples followed Jesus. Jesus asked them what they wanted; they simply wanted to know where He was staying. That was not an idle question. If He was their expected Messiah, they wanted to hear from Jesus Himself.

At His invitation, they stayed with Him the whole day, listening to Him. No longer were they satisfied with John's pointing to Jesus, they wanted to hear from Him directly. They set a pattern for us, not to settle for second hand information about Jesus.

40–42   Again, "the next day," John pointed out that Andrew was one of the two who followed Jesus the previous day. We assume the other disciple was John the Apostle (John A) the writer of this gospel, as he never refers to himself directly in the gospel account.

Andrew, after spending the previous day with Jesus, brought his brother Simon to Jesus by announcing his belief: "'We have found the Messiah' (that is, the Christ)." Time with Jesus spent in John's gospel will convince the open mind who Jesus really is.

Jesus forecast Simon's future by renaming him Peter, the "Rock," on which Christ would build His Church. But impulsive Peter would have some lessons to learn first during his ensuing three years with Jesus. He became a formidable leader in the Early Church and is a reminder God can use the most unlikely of us.

43–49   "The next day," Jesus left for Galilee, and found Philip in Bethsaida, about four days journey north of Jerusalem. He called Philip to follow Him. Philip in turn called his friend Nathanael, saying he had found "the one Moses wrote about in the Law, and about whom the prophets also wrote—Jesus of Nazareth, the son of Joseph."

Nathanael was a typical skeptic: "Nazareth! Can anything good come from there?" But on Philip's invitation to "come and see," He came to Jesus. Jesus saw Nathanael in a different light, "A true Israelite, in whom there is nothing false." Nathanael's skepticism ensured he would only settle for the truth from one he could trust. Nathanael questioned how Jesus knew him before Philip called him. The answers were enough to convince Nathanael Jesus was "the Son of God, You are the King of Israel."

50–51   Nathanael believed because of Jesus' foreknowledge of him, but that initial belief would lead to "greater things." Then Jesus declares the first of His critical truths ("I tell you the truth") sayings.

> *I tell you the truth, you shall see heaven open, and the angels of God ascending and descending on the Son of Man.*

It was important that Nathanael and those with him ("you" in this saying is plural in the original Greek) would understand more fully Jesus' identity and mission. In doing so, Jesus made an implicit reference to Jacob's vision recorded in Genesis 28:12–14.

The ladder Jacob saw was less important than the message that went with it. The promise given was a repeat of that given to Abraham, Genesis 12:2–3, 18:18, 22:17–18, to Isaac, Genesis 26:2–4, and now passed to Jacob. The relevant part of that promise for Nathanael was the promise to the patriarchs, "All peoples on earth will be blessed through you and your offspring," Genesis 28:14.

Jesus was that offspring who would bless "'all peoples." Jesus emphasized the promise to Nathanael, and the disciples with Him: they would become aware that all who receive Christ would see Jesus glorified by the Father for His willing sacrifice for humankind. Here, for the first time in John's gospel, Jesus refers to the "Son of Man," which had specific meaning for the Jews. See appendix B for the origin and use of this title Jesus used for Himself over eighty times in the gospels. Jesus Christ opened the way to heaven.

2

Jesus Reveals His Glory and Authority

Many people saw the miraculous signs He was doing and believed in His name. But Jesus would not entrust Himself to them, for He knew all men.

John 2:23-24

This chapter records two incidents: turning the water into wine and Jesus driving out the marketeers from the temple. In the first, Jesus shows His authority over nature. In the second incident, Jesus showed His authority over the temple and demonstrated what was not appropriate in the temple precincts, God's residence.

Jesus Turns Water into Wine

1-3   In this first event, Jesus showed His authority over the natural forces He created. Changing water into wine is a natural procedure, although nature takes time from falling rain to the fomented grape. Jesus simply sped the process up, like calming the storm.

Cana was about two days journey from the Galilee area, possibly from Nazareth where Jesus may have stayed with His mother. The wedding took place on the third day. Jesus' mother was there, and Jesus and His disciples were also invited. Having grown up in the area, many at the wedding party would know Him and, for the most part, it would be a friendly gathering; different from Jerusalem.

19

The wine ran out, an embarrassing position for the host. Mary turned to Jesus for help. Was she expecting a miracle, or some way Jesus could help–perhaps the disciples could buy some more? Jesus was, after all, her son who, in His earlier years, had helped around the house.

However, Mary knew who Jesus was; she had treasured in her heart what she had seen during His growing up years, Luke 2:51. She was content to raise the problem and leave the rest to Him.

4–5   At first reading, Jesus' response seems unnecessarily harsh, and most translations foster that view. The English translation cannot accurately portray Jesus' response. It was not disrespectful or sharp and the NIV's translation, "Dear woman," accurately shows more tenderness.

However, Jesus no longer addressed her as "mother," as her natural born son, but "woman," as her Lord. Now He was in a new relationship with her and all others. He was now the "Lamb of God," baptized in water and by the Holy Spirit.

Jesus desired to clarify how He would use His power and what His destiny was; not simply to help in an emergency. Others probably overheard the conversation as He announced, "My time [or hour] has not yet come." His time would be the cross and resurrection, as He pointed out several times during His ministry, 7:6, 30; 8:20; 12:23, 27; 13:1; 17:1.

This did not mean that the everyday things of life were unimportant to Him. That Jesus intervenes in the everyday affairs of life should not distract us from the primary purpose of His coming. Mary's answer was one of faith. She placed her dilemma before Him and left Him to work the answer out His way. She trusted Him: "Do whatever he tells you."

6–10   Six large jars, holding 20 or more gallons each, were nearby. The jars were for ceremonial washing, without which men and women could not participate in Jewish ceremonies.

Jesus called for the servants to fill them with water. Once filled, Jesus instructed the servants to take some to the master of the wedding banquet.

Not knowing where the wine had come from, the master of the banquet congratulated the bridegroom on keeping the best wine to last. Clearly, the normal practice was to bring cheaper wine later when alcohol from earlier wine had diminished the palate's ability to taste the difference.

The miracle was also an acted parable. Jesus' coming sacrifice would fulfill the ceremonial practices of the Old Testament. The later, "best" wine symbolized the new, greater life in Jesus Christ to which the sacrificial system pointed. Recall Jesus' parable of the wineskins, Matthew 9:17. Those unwilling to acknowledge Jesus could not accept Jesus' new wine; only lives made new could contain the new wine.

11   John records this miracle as the first sign Jesus performed that "revealed His glory." As noted in our introduction, John was more concerned with the meaning of Jesus' miracles than the miracles themselves. For John, each miracle revealed something of Jesus' divine identity—His glory.

But this first sign was a muted show of who He was. Very few were witnesses of it: His disciples, His mother, and a few servants. No flamboyant gestures pointed to Him, and no fanfare greeted the extraordinary event. A short quiet incident, like a door cracked open briefly, was all anyone saw. Yet implicit was a glimpse into the transcendent Lord of the universe and the humble authority with which He appeared on earth.

Jesus Clears the Temple

12–17   Jesus stayed with His family and disciples at Capernaum for a few days, before returning south to Jerusalem for the Passover. His reception there would not be like the pleasant surroundings and friends of the Cana wedding.

If Jesus reveled Himself in quiet humility at the Cana wedding, His approach to the temple marketeers was direct and forceful. The temple was God's dwelling place with men until He began to reign in their hearts, and Jesus would not tolerate the commercialization of space dedicated to God meeting with men. In this, His revelation of authority was open and deliberate for all to see, sufficiently to be challenged.

Only Jews could use the temple, but Gentiles could use the outer courtyard. That area became a place for commerce and not Gentile worship during Passover. Those who had traveled a distance needed to buy sacrificial animals there and moneychangers sold half-shekels for the temple fee. However, those selling made excessive charges; it was not only a market, but as Jesus observed elsewhere, "You have made it a den of robbers," Luke 19:46.

Jesus was angry. Anger is a God-given emotion to combat injustice, but needs to be controlled and constructive. His anger was not only to a market set up in a place of worship, but also at the exploitation of captive worshippers seeking to fulfill their obligations to God. However, Jesus' anger was controlled. He harmed no one, only upset their tables and drove out the animals. His anger was also constructive. Now a place was available for Gentile worshippers.

Jesus particularly denounced those selling doves. He carried an affinity with the poor all His ministry life, and the poorest could use birds as a substitute sacrifice for animals; even the poor were the object of exploitation by the marketers. His disciples recognized Jesus' fulfillment of the prophecy of Psalm 69:9 "Zeal for your house consumes me."

Of particular note, and easily missed, is Jesus' use of "My Father" in verse 16. The use of "Our Father," as Jesus taught in the Lord's Prayer, was a recognition that God is the Father of all—by creation for all humanity, or by conversion to become His children. But Jesus' use of "My Father" denoted a special relationship with God that the Jews recognized as assuming equality with God, see 5:16–18.

18–21   The Jews demanded to know where Jesus obtained His authority to clear the temple in this manner. In particular, they wanted a "miraculous sign" as proof of authority, as though Jesus was a traveling showman. They had probably heard of Jesus' miracles, as He had performed miracles while in Jerusalem, verse 23.

Jesus refused to comply with that frivolous request, and as He had done with His mother's request, pointed to His ultimate earthly death and resurrection as final proof of His divine authority. But He couched it in symbolic terms, similar to His parables, "Destroy this temple, and I will raise it again in three days."

The Jews, mistakenly, or deliberately, assumed Jesus was talking about the temple itself. The temple, still incomplete, had been building forty-six years to that date. Jesus could rebuild it in three days? With the Jews knowledge of the Scriptures, they should have recognized Him and not required a sign, but throughout His ministry they refused to believe Him. Even the disciples would recognize the meaning of Jesus' words only after His resurrection, but they would confirm their previous belief in Him.

22–25   Many also believed on Him when they saw the miraculous signs He did. But there was a difference. Some simply believed in the miracles, but His disciples recognized the signs were only a pointer to Jesus the Messiah.

Jesus was aware of the difference. Once Jesus made the claims of the Gospel clear, those with superficial faith in the miracles would fall away, and Jesus could not rely on their profession of belief. Eventually many of them would call for His crucifixion. His disciples and others followed Him, not because He performed miracles, but because they came to trust the signs of His deity they saw displayed.

23

3

Jesus Teaches Nicodemus' and John Witnesses to Jesus

"For God so loved the world that He gave His one and only Son, that whoever believes in Him shall not perish but have eternal life,"

John 3:16

The previous chapter illustrated Jesus' reaction to pleasure in a social group in their joyful wedding celebration, but also His anger at those who abused and exploited God's provision for their own ends. In this chapter, Jesus reacts with care and precision to a genuine seeker after the truth. The chapter divides easily into two parts: first Jesus' interaction with Nicodemus and His witness to the truth, and second, John's own witness to Jesus Christ.

Jesus Witnesses to Nicodemus

1-2   Nicodemus was a member of the Jewish ruling council, the Sanhedrin, and probably came to Jesus during darkness for fear of his fellow rulers. He came with genuine questions, not the prejudice of those who had questioned John, and later questioned Jesus.

Nicodemus' questions sought much the same as John's questioners, wondering who Jesus really was. At least he realized He was "a teacher who has come from God," promoted by Jesus' miracles. But as we saw previously, belief in miracles was also insufficient, 2:23. Satan's followers can also perform miracles, Matthew 24:24, 2 Thessalonians 2:2, and Revelation 13:13. Even the Pharisees claimed Jesus drove out demons by Satan's "Prince of demons," Matthew 12:24.

3–6   Jesus taught Nicodemus that following a pattern of lawful behaviour is insufficient to enter heaven. New life is only through regeneration, new birth, by the Holy Spirit, as we believe in Jesus Christ. Faith is an "affair of the heart," not outward show, see Matthew 23:25–26.

Nicodemus believed, as the Jewish leadership and many believe today, in works-righteousness. He considered Jesus' miracles proof of God's ministry—a glimpse of the Kingdom of Heaven in Jesus. Jesus may have seen emptiness in Nicodemus' heart. Jesus cut across Nicodemus' beliefs with the first of three declarations in this chapter of critical truths, signifying the basic important truth Nicodemus, and indeed all, needed to know and believe.

I tell you the truth, no one can see the Kingdom of God unless he is born again.

Jesus emphasized the truth that the only way into God's Kingdom was by being born again. Nicodemus' answer showed his dependence on worldly, natural affairs. For the Jews, work here and now received the favour of God. Thus, physical birth or rebirth was all Nicodemus could conceive. In explanation, Jesus stated a second critical truth.

I tell you the truth, no one can enter the Kingdom of God unless he is born of water and the Spirit.

Jesus stressed the second birth as a work of regeneration of the Holy Spirit, separate from, but as essential as, physical birth. Meaningful and enduring works are an *outcome* of regeneration by the Holy Spirit, not the *means* of entering God's Kingdom.

Water in verse 5 has been interpreted several ways. Some have suggested it referred to the ritual of water baptism necessary for salvation. However, the New Testament never indicates any ritual saves. Ritual, especially baptism, is an outward confirmation of inward belief.

Another suggestion, closer to the truth, is that water here represents the purification of those who accept Jesus Christ. But most likely, it simply referred to the mother's water breaking to ease childbirth. Note the parallel with "flesh" giving birth to flesh in verse 6. But the Holy Spirit gives birth to spiritual life.

7–8   Jesus opened these verses with "you should not be surprised," at the necessity of being born again, probably anticipating Nicodemus' ignorance later in verses 9 and 10. Particularly in verse 8, Jesus revealed we have no control of the work of the Spirit, who like the wind, "blows wherever it pleases."

A play on the words "spirit" and "wind," not obvious in English, is that both are translated from the Greek word pneuma, making the comparison between the two even tighter. But the message Jesus had for Nicodemus is that although we cannot tell what the Spirit does or where He goes, He leaves a recognizable trail.

This may have drawn Nicodemus to Jesus. That is why those who are led by the Spirit are a mystery to others. The trail of evidence of the Spirit's work is visible even though they cannot understand it.

9–12   Obviously, Nicodemus did not understand it: "How can this be?" Jesus rebuked him for his ignorance as a teacher in Israel; in this case for his ignorance of the working of the Holy Spirit within human life. For the third time to Nicodemus, Jesus asserted a further critical truth.

> I tell you the truth, we speak of what we know, and we testify to what we have seen, but still you people do not accept our testimony.

Jesus and His disciples spoke of what they knew and had seen of spiritual things. In Jesus case, His authority also stemmed from His knowledge of heaven from whence He came, but "still you people do not accept our testimony." As John had stated earlier, "He came to that which was His own, but His own did not receive Him," 1:11.

Jesus spoke of "earthly things," those events of the Spirit's work on earth. Note particularly Ezekiel 36:25–27, and Jeremiah 33:33–34. If Nicodemus could not comprehend the work of the Spirit on earth, how could he understand what was taking place in the heavenly realms?

13–15   At this point, Jesus attested to His heavenly origin. For the second time in John's gospel, Jesus referred to Himself as the "Son of Man." Jesus used this title here to affirm His claim as witness to the basic truth of life, for as the One from heaven, He spoke as the real source of all things, clearly stated by John as he opened his gospel, 1:1–4.

Jesus explained His personal authority. He is the One who knows heaven and its requirements because He came from there. Thus, He is able to speak of things in heaven, and their affect on earthly life. In particular, He predicted His crucifixion–being "lifted up"–by comparing it with the snake in the wilderness, Numbers 21:5–9. As those who saw the snake were healed of its bite, so forgiveness of sin and eternal life come to those who believe and accept Jesus' sacrifice.

Nicodemus and his fellow Jews should have recognized Jesus. The Old Testament Scriptures spoke of Him, but if they misunderstood or misinterpreted them, they should have recognized Jesus by the authority He wielded. At least Nicodemus recognized it, even if he did not understand it. The Jews' ignorance, or deliberate rejection of Him, led to rejection of Jesus' declaration of the truth.

16–18   In the deservedly well-known text of verse 16, Jesus clearly stated the purpose of His entry into the world. He came to save from God's wrath those who come to Him. He came as a sacrifice of atonement–God "gave His one and only Son," that God's wrath abiding on all sin could be dispelled for all those who believe in Jesus Christ. Jesus doubled down on this. His purpose was not judgment, but to save the world. As John pointed out, He had the authority as "the Lamb of God who takes away the sin of the world," 1:29.

But for those who disbelieve and reject the salvation offered by Jesus' sacrifice, they remain in their sin, condemned by God, and will perish. Note Jesus' emphasis on belief or refusal to believe. Belief as the means of release from the wrath of God occurs 5 times in verses 15–18, and again in verse 36.

19–21   John states as a "verdict," the judgment handed down from the Court of Heaven. Light, used as a metaphor for truth, "has come into the world." While the realms of light and darkness exist in the heavenly realms, they exist physically on earth. Just as a thief usually works under cover of darkness, so those who continue in evil avoid the light of Christ.

We live by truth, which is Jesus Christ, 14:6. Truth exposes evil, and the light of Christ exposes our inner selves and our tendency for independence from God. We live by the truth as we come into the light of Christ, and what we are becoming "has been done through God." Our salvation from God's wrath is all His work.

John's Testimony of Jesus

22–26   Following Jesus' encounter with Nicodemus, He spent time with His disciples and began to baptize, although the disciples baptized for Him, 4:2. John continued to baptize also, but some of John's disciples raised questions.

First, they argued about ceremonial washing. They probably believed how it was done and who was baptizing would determine how effective the ritual was. They, like Nicodemus, believed the ritual system purified them, whereas Jesus had already advised Nicodemus that only new birth–believing and receiving Jesus through regeneration by the Holy Spirit–brought purification.

Second, John's disciples were jealous for him because many were leaving John and following Jesus. Then, as now,

29

squabbles over status frequently plague the advancement of the Kingdom of God. Envy and Jealousy have no place before the supremacy of Christ.

27–30 John understood this position clearly. All of us can only operate within the mandate God has given us. John clearly stated in 1:21–27, he was not the Christ and here reaffirmed it. He was only the "best man," awaiting the "Bridegroom" and John's joy was not in his own success, but the coming of the Bridegroom, Jesus the Messiah.

John also understood his work was to glorify Christ. In fact, the indwelling Spirit's work is to glorify Christ, 16:12–16. Thus, John considered his role should diminish in favour of Jesus Christ. John nailed it down: The call and enabling of the Spirit were not for his own glory; John would decrease, as the Bridegroom increased.

31–36 In these verses, John punches out the deity of Christ. He witnessed to Jesus as "the One who comes from above is above all," and "the One who comes from heaven is above all." Thus Jesus' knowledge and witness of heavenly things is credible. But the one "from the earth" only understands the things of earth, see 1 Corinthians 2:11–13. However, the majority, then, as now, refused to accept it.

Conversely, John claimed that those who accept the witness of Jesus Christ, the One from heaven, are also witnesses to the truth of God in Jesus Christ. They recognize truth by the illuminating presence of the indwelling Spirit given "without limit" to those who believe. See 1 Corinthians 2:8–10.

Repeating Jesus' words in 3:16–18, John pointed out that Jesus has full authority from the Father, not just as Saviour, but also as Judge, 5:27. Belief in Him guarantees eternal life; not in the future, as the Jews believed, but immediately for the believer here on earth.

But for those who reject Jesus Christ, there is no other option but to face God's wrath. God is actively opposed to evil, and His wrath will not fade with time. God will finally eradicate all evil. There is no permanent life outside of Jesus Christ.

4

The Woman at the Well and the Official's Son Healed

"Whoever drinks the water I give him will never thirst. Indeed, the water I give him will become in him a spring of water welling up to eternal life."

John 4:14

Previous chapters recorded interactions Jesus had with individuals and groups. This chapter deals with two further individuals Jesus ministered to: the Samaritan woman at the well, and the official whose son was dying. The stories of the Samaritan woman and Nicodemus show striking differences, illustrating Jesus' compassion for both extremes. Jesus compassion crossed all levels of society; He was a master at cross-cultural communication.

Nicodemus	The Samaritan Woman
Came to Jesus at night	Met Jesus at midday
Initiated conversation with Jesus	Conversation initiated by Jesus
Thorough knowledge of Scripture	Biblically illiterate
Very moral and religious	Considered immoral
A highly respected man	An outcast woman
Rich and influential	Poor and powerless

Named	Nameless
Slow to believe and receive	Quick to believe and receive
Confessed Jesus later	Confessed Jesus immediately

A brief summary of the background causing animosity between the Jews and Samaritans is helpful. Solomon, despite his wisdom, turned from following God and the nation was taken from him and divided in two, 1 Kings 11:11-13. The southern kingdom was named Judah, and the remaining tribes to the north became the nation of Israel, also called Samaria.

In BC 722, the Assyrians overran Israel (Samaria), deported many inhabitants, and replaced them with peoples from other lands. This resulted in both mixed bloodlines and mixed worship, so the Jews considered Samaria apostate, see 2 Kings 17: 21-33. Thus, the descendants of Samaria became the hated Samaritans.

To stop the Samaritans going to Jerusalem, the kings of Israel changed the Pentateuch (Genesis to Deuteronomy), made mount Gerizim the place of worship, and built a temple there. They continued their worship of God, however deficient, still considering themselves descendants of Jacob. This explains the woman's confusion in verse 20.

The Woman at Jacob's Well

1-6 The Jewish leadership was suspicious of both John and Jesus. When the Jews noticed Jesus gained more followers than John, Jesus took His disciples north to Galilee to avoid a premature confrontation. That would come later.

Samaria lay between Judea and Galilee. The shortest route to Galilee was through it, but devout Jews would cross the Jordan River and go around Samaria, for the "Jews had no dealings with the Samaritans." However, Jesus meant to go through Samaria, not because it was the shorter route, but to show Himself as the God of the Samaritans as well as the

Jews. Here was the beginning of His greater ministry to the Gentile races.

Jesus was tired. Despite being God incarnate, He suffered the same ills as a normal human, and He rested by Jacob's well. It was noon, the hottest part of the day, but Jesus had no means to draw water.

7–12   Jesus' disciples went into town to get food, so Jesus was alone. He asked a Samaritan woman who came to draw water, if she would give Him a drink. The woman was surprised Jesus spoke to her. Normally, no Jew would talk to a Samaritan, nor would a Jewish man open a conversation with a woman, especially if she was alone. Furthermore, Jews considered the Samaritans unclean so they would not normally use the dishes used by the Samaritans, in this case the woman's bucket.

Like His direct confrontation with Nicodemus, in response to the woman's question, Jesus went straight to the woman's need–for living water, which He was able to dispense. Already, in His conversation with the woman, Jesus was intimating His identity; Jesus labelled living water a "gift of God." The Greek word used here is used in the New Testament as the gracious gift of God, not simply a gift.

The woman's rambling response showed her misunderstanding of the offer Jesus made. "Living water" to her was stream-fed water, rather than stagnant water from a cistern. The Samaritans revered Jacob, and she accused Jesus of assuming Himself greater than Jacob.

13–18   Jesus tried to explain to the woman that the water He offered was the water of life that would satisfy her inward desires not her physical thirst, the indwelling Spirit, see 7:37–39. But she was still stuck in physical thinking: "so I won't get thirsty and have to keep coming here to draw water."

Jesus tried another tack. "Go, call your husband and come back." He opened a dialog that would reveal His full identity. She hedged, simply stating she had no husband. If she was beginning to think of Jesus as some sort of prophet, she did not wish to reveal her questionable past and put Him off.

But Jesus, then as now, was concerned with disposing of sin, not hiding it. His next comments showed He knew all about her, yet continued speaking with her. She had married five husbands and was now living common law, an immoral woman in Jewish eyes.

19–26 Now followed an exchange in which the woman defended the claim there are many ways to God, a direct contention to justify her current practice. The woman assumed Jesus as a prophet as He knew so much about her. She explained that although the Jews maintain worship must be at the temple in Jerusalem, the Samaritans have their temple at mount Gerizim from where they worship.

But as with Nicodemus, Jesus cut across her claims. Location was not the arbiter of genuine worship, but worship from the heart and in truth. With Jesus' coming, worship would not be from any specific location. But Jesus also maintained that truth was also a basis for acceptable worship, and He was the source of truth, "You Samaritans worship what you do not know; we worship what we do know, for salvation is from the Jews." Jesus maintained salvation was from the Jews as Jesus, who would provide the sacrifice to do away with sin, was a Jew.

Jesus also predicted the time when the Holy Spirit would indwell the temple of the human body and so worship would be through the spirit. He went further, saying the time "*has now come* when the true worshipers will worship the Father in spirit and truth," (my emphasis).

The woman still questioned Jesus' claim pointing, as she thought, to a higher authority, the Messiah. "When He comes, He will explain everything to us." This prompted Jesus to reveal himself, "*I*, who speak to you, *am* He." This is the first instance in John's gospel of the emphatic use of "I am," as Jesus identified Himself with the "I am" of the Old Testament.

27–33   The disciples returned and found Jesus in deep conversation with a woman, in particular a Samaritan woman. They said nothing, fearful of Jesus' ability to reverse their arguments. But the woman, amazed by Jesus' intimate knowledge of her life, now seriously considered Jesus as the Messiah: "Could this be the Christ?" She called her neighbours and friends to come and meet Him.

The disciples had only been with Jesus a short time. They were apparently still as earthly minded as Nicodemus and the Samaritan woman. When they urged Him to eat, He told them He had food they knew nothing about. They could only surmise someone else had brought Him food.

34–38   As with Nicodemus, 3:10–21, and here, Jesus used this opportunity for teaching, and He opened up the idea that that spiritual food had sustained Him. Jesus' food was "to do the will of Him who sent me and to finish His work."

Recall Jesus' words to Satan when Jesus was fasting and hungry: "Man does not live on bread alone, but on every word that comes from the mouth of God," Matthew 4:4. Physical food provides existence. God's Word creates life. Sometimes, exhilaration on fulfilling God's call replaces physical hunger– at least for a time.

Jesus continued teaching on sowing and reaping, indicating He was talking about spiritual things, harvesting "the crop for eternal life." But the spiritual harvest differed from the natural harvest. The natural harvest depended on the seasons, but the spiritual harvest was already ripe; the spiritual work of sowing and reaping continue alongside each other.

Sowing is laborious work, often with no apparent result. Reaping builds on another's work, and is a time of rejoicing. Seed sown faithfully will have its harvest and sower and reaper will rejoice together. For the sower will rejoice in seeing men and women turn to God. But it is also the reward of those who have labored faithfully in sowing the word. Compare Psalm 126:6, "He who goes out weeping, carrying seed to sow, will return with songs of joy, carrying sheaves with him."

39–42   Because of Jesus' talk with the Samaritan woman, and her witness, many from the town believed in Him. Note the sequence of belief. The woman's report was their first basis of belief. They began believing because of the woman's testimony, or as we have seen, others believed on seeing the miracles Jesus performed. If we remain in this state of belief, dependent on the words or works of others for our faith, we are God's grandchildren.

But the Samaritans went further. They wanted to know Him better for themselves, and at their request, He stayed with them for two days. Firm faith depends on knowing Jesus personally, not just based on someone else's witness. This paved the way for the last and necessary stage. "Now we have heard for ourselves, and we know that this man really is the Saviour of the world." Now they became His children of God, no longer His grandchildren.

43–45   After staying with the Samaritans for two days, Jesus and the disciples journeyed on to Galilee. Here John points up a discrepancy: Jesus had previously stated a prophet has no honour in his own country, yet the Galileans of His home territory welcomed Him. Apparently, it seems they were interested in His miracles seen at Cana, not in His claims.

Recall John's words that He came to His own but they did not receive Him, 1:10–11. We have already seen the Jews hounding both John and Jesus previously. Even those in His home town of Nazareth rejected Him when He claimed to be the fulfillment of Isaiah 61:1–2, see Luke 4:16–30.

Jesus Heals the Official's Son

46–50   Jesus' fame was well known, even among the aristocracy. Jesus again visited Cana, only fifteen miles from Capernaum. The man in these verses was a royal official, a

Jew from Herod's palace. Position or importance does not shield us from pain and this man's son was dying. He made the journey to Cana to seek healing from Jesus for his son.

Jesus' answer seems unduly harsh. Perhaps the official was hoping to see a miracle as evidence of who Jesus was. Jesus' answer, not just to the official but to all who heard Him (you is plural here), confirmed he did not need to see a miracle to believe. As we have seen, miracles may be a step to faith, but cannot establish firm, permanent faith.

Besides, the official was less interested in discussing faith than having his son healed. He asked again for Jesus to come and heal his son. Jesus, sensing his faith told him "You may go. Your son will live." The man returned satisfied, trusting in Jesus' words. Those were words of power, not simple prophecy.

51–54   It was not until the next day, as the official was returning home, he learned that his son was healed at the exact time Jesus had said. This miracle confirmed Jesus divine power to reverse the progress toward death. The official's faith caused his whole household to believe. Jesus did not have to be present to perform this miracle, nor does He need to be physically present with us to be involved in our lives.

Although Jesus had performed miracles elsewhere, 2:23 and 3:2, this was the second sign of Jesus' identity John records, both of which took place in Cana of Galilee.

5

The Lame Man Healed and Jesus Proclaimed His Identity

Whoever hears my word and believes Him who sent me has eternal life and will not be condemned; he has crossed over from death to life.

John 5:24

We left Jesus in Galilee in chapter 4, and now He returned to Jerusalem for a Jewish feast, although we are not told which feast He attended.

Set back in Jerusalem, this chapter has two sections. The first is the story of the lame man healed by Jesus. In the second section Jesus gives extended teaching supporting His identity in response to persecution from the Jews for healing on the Sabbath.

Healing at the Pool

1–8 Back in Jerusalem, Jesus visited the Bethesda pools where many sick, lame, and paralyzed lay. It should be noted that some translations include verse 4—omitted in the NIV and newer translations—indicating that when an angel disturbs the water, the first into the water is healed. However, this explanation is not in the earliest manuscripts, and may have been added later to explain verse 7.

However, the important story is Jesus' healing of the man,

especially on the Sabbath. Jesus asked this man, incapacitated for thirty-eight years, if he wished to be healed. A strange question, but some invalids may have gained handouts because of their sickness, and had no prospects of income if they were healed.

The implied answer is yes, as the man clearly had hopes of healing up to that day. Jesus responded with a simple command: "Get up! Pick up your mat and walk." There is no mention of faith on the man's part, although Jesus frequently referred to faith as a trigger for healing, it was clearly not mandatory. Certainly raising a person from the dead could not demand faith. However, obedience is a sign of faith. The man obeyed Jesus, and became whole as he stood up.

9–15 Immediately the opposition began. The Jews told the man he was sinning because carrying his mat was against the Sabbath law. However, it was not the law that forbade it but the Jews' narrow interpretation of the law. The man referred to the one who made him whole and who gave him instructions to carry his mat, but did not know who He was.

Later, Jesus found the man in the temple, and noted he was well. Continuing in obedience maintains faith and healing. But Jesus warned that continuing in sin would have worse consequences. Then the man went to the Jews and reported that Jesus had healed him and told him to carry his mat.

Jesus' Response to the Jews

16–18 We noted previously the continuing opposition of the Jews (referring to the Jewish leadership) for healing on the Sabbath. Apparently, "Jesus was doing these things on the Sabbath"; it was His ongoing practice and led the Jews to harass Him on the subject. The remainder of this chapter is a response by Jesus to that opposition. The Jews provided two reasons for their displeasure.

First, the Jews forbade work on the Sabbath, which in their view included healing. In response, Jesus said God is always working, even on the Sabbath. He provides sun, rain, and wind every day, and His compassion does not rest on the Sabbath. Compare Jesus' words in Luke 6:9: "I ask you, which is lawful on the Sabbath: to do good or to do evil, to save life or to destroy it?"

Second, Jesus called God "My Father," not "our Father." They understood this as a claim that made Jesus equal with God. For them, who believed Jesus was simply a man, that was blasphemy and punishable by death. So they "tried all the harder to kill Him."

Some would suggest they only thought that was what Jesus was claiming. However, both the Jews and Jesus were steeped in the culture of the time, and it is more reasonable to assume they understood exactly what Jesus was saying better than those of us living two thousand years later.

19–23   In response to this incident, Jesus proclaimed the first of three critical truth statements in this chapter.

I tell you the truth, the Son can do nothing by Himself;
He can do only what He sees His Father doing, because
whatever the Father does the Son also does.

Not only is the Son the exact representation of the Father, Hebrews 1:3, Jesus also declared to the Jews that He exactly replicates the work of the Father. Simply put, Jesus revealed Himself as the Son of God by fulfilling the Father's work on earth.

Conversely, Jesus condemned the Jews' disobedience to God by coercing their extreme interpretations of the law and forbidding healing on the Sabbath. Strangely, the Jews did not deny Jesus' healing of the man. From John's point of view, this was a sign of Jesus' identity and authority, which should have led them, like Nicodemus, to enquire more deeply about who Jesus was.

Jesus confirmed that the wonders He performed—even on the Sabbath—came from, and were, the desire of God. Furthermore, because the Father loves the Son, He would display even greater things. Note the following attributes

43

Jesus claims here for Himself that confirm His deity. "The Father raises the dead," and the Jews believed this power was God's alone. But Jesus would display this power during His ministry..

The Son received the Father's power to give life, not only for human existence, but also spiritual life for eternity. Furthermore, the Father entrusted all judgment to the Son. Again, the Jews believed this was God's prerogative alone, but Jesus claimed it for Himself.

Finally, Jesus proclaimed that to honour the Son is to honour the Father. God is dishonoured when Jesus Christ, sent by the Father, is dishonoured. The Jews' refusal to recognize Jesus as their Messiah from God was a direct indictment of the Jews' failure to know God.

24–26   In these verses, Jesus declared two more critical truth statements confirming His authority over life and death. The first proclaims:

> I tell you the truth, whoever hears my word and believes Him who sent me has eternal life and will not be condemned; he has crossed over from death to life.

Eternal life depends on belief, both in who the Son is, and the words He has spoken. There are two options, to believe and have life, or not to believe and be condemned. We are all initially in a state of condemnation and death, Ephesians 2:4-5, but "because of His great love for us, God, who is rich in mercy, made us alive with Christ even when we were dead in transgressions—it is by grace you have been saved." Those who believe "cross over from death to life."

Secondly, Jesus emphasized the critical truth that all the dead will hear the voice of the Son of God.

> I tell you the truth, a time is coming and has now come when the dead will hear the voice of the Son of God and those who hear will live.

To hear in this context is not just to be aware of His voice, but to respond to it. Note the instructions in Revelation chapters 2 and 3: "He who has an ear, let him hear what the

Spirit says to the churches." For, as Jesus said in verse 21, the Son has the ability to give life, even to those alive, yet are "dead in your transgressions and sins," Ephesians 2:1, because the Father granted it to Him.

27–30   In these verses, Jesus returned to the subject of judgment raised in verse 22. Jesus now changed His title to the Son of Man. All Jews understood this reference to their coming Messiah, the Son of Man, whose status was predicted in Daniel 7:13–14. Note especially verse 14: "He was given authority, glory and sovereign power; all peoples, nations and men of every language worshiped Him. His dominion is an everlasting dominion that will not pass away, and His kingdom is one that will never be destroyed." See Appendix B for more detail on the Son of Man.

With that authority, *all* will hear His voice and come from the grave to stand before Him. Each will be judged according to good or evil. Evil, in context, is to reject Jesus, God's Messiah, see verse. 24; recall also John 3:18. "Whoever believes in Him is not condemned, but whoever does not believe stands condemned already because he has not believed in the name of God's one and only Son."

To reject Jesus Christ is to remain in sin and be judged accordingly. Belief in Him erases our sin by His blood. Ephesians 2:13, "Now in Christ Jesus you who once were far away have been brought near through the blood of Christ." An honourable judge is one who acts fairly. Christ's judgment is just, for He judges as He hears from the Father, and Jesus' foremost desire is to please Him.

31–40   In these verses, Jesus listed witnesses to His person and identity. He accepted the Jewish position one cannot testify about oneself, a logical position at all times; there has to be a valid witness. Jesus claimed there is one—presumably referring to the Father, and He expands on how the Father testified to Him in the following verses.

Jesus clearly stated human testimony did not establish His

identity. But as a beginning for the Jews to understand His witnesses, He mentioned John as a witness. John clearly testified who Jesus was, and the Jews accepted John's message "for a time."

But of greater significance, the work Jesus did testified to Him, because it was the Father's work. If the Jews really knew the Father, they would have recognized Jesus sent from God because He did the Father's work.

Furthermore, the Word testifies to Him. Although the Jews had never seen or heard God physically, He had spoken to them through His Word. But their view of Scripture, biased toward the Law, missed it's predictions of the Saviour coming to free people from the law. Recall Jesus' teaching about Himself from Scripture, Luke 24:25–27, 45–48. See Appendix F for prophecies of Jesus' first coming Jesus referenced from the Old Testament.

The Jews sought the Word for eternal life, but Jesus condemned them because they were ignorant of the Scriptures that pointed to Jesus who alone could offer them life, and so rejected Him as the source of life.

41–44 Jesus refused to accept praise from men. He knew their heart, and like today, most men endeavour to praise Him for perceived attributes that are untrue. In that, they prove they do not love God who is truth, but prefer their own assessment of the truth about Him.

Again, then as today, they prefer to accept the false assumptions of those who tell them what they want to hear. As Paul reminds Timothy, "For the time will come when men will not put up with sound doctrine. Instead, to suit their own desires, they will gather around them a great number of teachers to say what their itching ears want to hear," 2 Timothy 4:3.

Jesus reminds His listeners they cannot believe in Him as long as they accept praise from each other and deny themselves the praise that comes from God.

45–47   Although judgment would come from Jesus, their accuser would be Moses. They claimed Moses was their source of truth. However, Jesus highlighted the truth that Moses looked forward to the coming of the Messiah, Genesis to Deuteronomy. As far back as Genesis 49:10, the ultimate King of Israel would come from the descendents of Judah. Other references are included in Appendix F.

The Jews' failure to believe these predictions by Moses meant that they could not and would not believe Jesus.

6

Jesus Feeds the Five Thousand and Teaches on the Bread of Life

I am the bread of life. He who comes to me will never go hungry, and he who believes in me will never be thirsty.

John 6:35

This chapter is the longest in John's gospel, but is almost all concerned with one theme: Jesus is the Bread of Life. The feeding of the five thousand is only a prelude to Jesus' teaching on this subject. The chapter divides easily into three sections. The first records feeding the five thousand, the second Jesus walking on the water. The final section, the longest, covers Jesus' teaching on the Bread of Life.

Feeding the five thousand is the only miracle recorded in all four gospels. Each gospel has detail that is missing in the others, thus, it is helpful to glean some facts from Matthew 14:13-21, Mark 6:32-44, and Luke 9:10-17, to add depth to John's version. Before feeding the five thousand, Jesus learned Herod had beheaded John the Baptist (Matthew and Mark).

Jesus Feeds the Five Thousand

1-4   This chapter occurs "some time after this,"–the events of the last chapter–and Jesus had left Jerusalem for Galilee. Jesus, wanted to be alone, partly to grieve the loss of John the Baptist, but also that He and the disciples could rest.

49

They took a boat and rowed the four miles across the Sea of Galilee to a solitary place near Bethsaida (Luke), the hometown of Philip and Andrew, 1:44.

Verse 4 notes it was near the time of the Passover. Passover also indicates it was the spring of the year, and Mark mentions "green grass." Here at the base of what we now know as the Golan Heights, Jesus and the disciples found a huge crowd had followed them. The crowd had taken the longer route on land around the head of the sea, a distance of about nine miles. Some who came to meet Him were there because of the miracles they had seen Jesus perform.

5–9   Seeing the crowd, Mark 6:34 says Jesus had compassion on them "because they were like sheep without a shepherd." Matthew tells us that He healed their diseases and Mark adds that He also taught them despite His tiredness. John omits these facts and gets straight to feeding the five thousand.

As evening closed in, Jesus asked, "Where shall we buy bread for these people to eat?" In their responses, Philip mentioned the large cost of feeding them, and Andrew who found the loaves and fishes lamented it was insufficient. But Jesus was testing them. The Greek word for test, peirasmos, means both test and trial. It emphasized the trial placed before the disciples was also a test of faith.

We can't help admiring the young lad for his willingness to sacrifice his lunch to Jesus. His was an exemplary faith, willing to give rather than take from Jesus like the rest of the crowd, verse 26.

10–13   This passage is interesting because of the organized way Jesus fed the crowd. The men were told to sit; the other gospels state they were seated by hundreds and fifties, and the men were fed.

What about feeding the women and children mentioned by Matthew? One assumes the men received enough to feed the families with them, perhaps single men feeding women and children with no family accompanying them.

But the four evangelists report *all* had sufficient, even to leaving twelve baskets of fragments over. Jesus cared enough, not only to feed the crowd, but also to avoid waste. Compare this with good food thrown out today by supermarkets and families while so many in the world are starving.

14–15   This miracle was enough to convince the crowd Jesus was probably "the Prophet who is to come into the world." As He had miraculously fed everyone, so He could become king and liberate them from the Roman occupation, and a tyrannical Jewish king.

While the Jews and Herod wanted Jesus killed, this crowd supported Him. But it was for their own purposes, not the purpose He came for, see verse 27. Now, as Jesus dispersed the crowd, He finally gained the solitude He sought on the mountainside.

Jesus Walks on the Water

16–21   It may seem strange that the disciples would take off and leave Jesus behind. But Mark tells us that Jesus "made His disciples get into the boat and go on ahead of Him." He needed the time to be alone.

The disciples rowed but the sea became rough, and "the wind was against them" (Mark). The boat was "in the middle of the lake" between 3.00 and 6.00 a.m. indicated by Mark as the third watch of the night.

Remember, despite their adversity, they were obeying the Lord's command. Even Jesus' appearance walking on the water seemed ominous. Adversity did not mean they were out of the Lord's will. Quite the reverse; as the Son did the Father's will He stirred up opposition and was killed for it. Eventually His disciples encountered the same opposition.

Jesus was aware of their predicament, and He met them at their point of need. His appearance and help came in a most unexpected way. As if to emphasize the completeness of

51

Jesus' intervention with the disciples' dilemma, John, who was in the boat, reports: "immediately the boat reached the shore where they were heading."

The Questions

22–27   Earlier verses note the crowd knew the disciples had departed in the only boat, so their first question was how Jesus reached Capernaum. That was something only He and His disciples knew, and probably Jesus wanted it to stay that way. Walking on the water was something the Jews would not readily accept, and even elicit ridicule.

Jesus sidestepped the question, "When did you get here?" as irrelevant; He wanted to teach a critical truth They had come because He had fed their stomachs, not even necessarily because they observed His miracles. Seeking food for eternal life was a greater need and evoked a critical truth.

I tell you the truth, you are looking for me, not because you saw miraculous signs but because you ate the loaves and had your fill. Do not work for food that spoils, but for food that endures to eternal life, which the Son of Man will give you. On Him God the Father has placed His seal of approval.

Clearly, the crowd had missed the significance of the sign of feeding the five thousand. The sign pointed to Jesus, but not as an earthly king they sought, but a king whose "Kingdom is not of this world," 18:36. He wanted to give them heavenly bread. Earthly, physical bread, would eventually mould and rot, but the heavenly bread He, the Son of Man, offered them was eternal.

Jesus called Himself the Son of Man. That title would send the Jews back to Daniel 7:13–14, to the origin of the title. This was the inauguration of the authority and power of the Son of Man to receive worship from all nations and receive His eternal kingdom. Appendix B gives a further explanation of the meaning of Son of Man.

Furthermore, at His baptism, Jesus was sealed with the

descending Spirit and His Father's approval, "This is my Son, whom I love; with Him I am well pleased," Matthew 17:5. Jesus was the one on whom "God the Father has placed His seal of approval."

Jesus was clearly laying again the groundwork to confirm His equality with God, recall 5:18. This divine authority undergirded and confirmed the truth He continued to teach in the remainder of this chapter.

28–29   Naturally, the Jews wanted that approval of God that Jesus claimed for Himself, so they asked the second question: "What must we do to do the works God requires?" The question betrayed their tradition that "works" (in the plural) were a way to please God.

However, in His answer, Jesus used the singular, "work," to describe what was necessary: "To believe in the One [God] has sent." This was not a new message Jesus was proclaiming,; recall previous passages, 1:12–13; 3:16–18, 36; 4:14, 42; 5:21, 24–25. Jesus forcefully declared acceptance by God is through belief in Jesus Christ, and not by religious or moral performance.

30–33   Why did this crowd ask this question: "What miraculous sign then will you give that we may see it and believe you?" Had they not seen the miracle themselves fed by a boy's meager lunch? Perhaps some new members of the crowd had not seen the miracle of feeding the five thousand. Their need for some sort of proof is the plague that infests the non-Christian world today—without proof I will not believe.

However, if proof was available faith would not be necessary. Jesus wanted, and still seeks, those who will believe in Him without some miraculous conjuring trick that will fade like the morning mist. Some will eventually wonder if the miracle actually happened; others will find a "natural" cause for the miraculous.

To reinforce their belief that proof of Jesus' authority was necessary, the Jews referred back to Moses, whose miracle of manna proved Moses' authority. They wanted a continuous miracle like the manna provided for forty years, still thinking in earthly terms. Here Jesus referred them to His second critical truth in this chapter.

I tell you the truth, it is not Moses who has given you the bread from heaven, but it is my Father who gives you the true bread from heaven. For the bread of God is He who comes down from heaven and gives life to the world.

Moses had not provided the manna in the desert; it had come from God's hand in heaven. Jesus Christ names Himself the true bread, also from heaven, who came to give life to the world.

The Bread of Life

34–40   The fogged minds of the Jews at this point simply asked for the bread Jesus offered. But they were still operating on the earthly plane. Like the woman who wanted "living" water so she would not need to return to the well, so those questioning Jesus simply wanted to have "living" bread to avoid having to go to the store for more.

So far, Jesus had been offering the bread from heaven, but now Jesus declared, "I *am* the bread of life." Here, for the second time in John's gospel, Jesus uses the emphatic form of "I *am*," having previously used it to the woman at the well, 4:26.

In this passage Jesus addressed a discussion that would arise fifteen hundred years later, and which is still a source of discussion today: has God chosen us "before the creation of the world," Ephesians 1:4, and thus decreed those who would be saved. Alternatively, are we saved by our choice to believe in Jesus? "Whoever believes in him shall not perish but have eternal life," 3:16.

In answer, Jesus indicated both–seeming opposites–are true. Note "He who comes" and "he who believes" in verse 35, and "everyone who looks to the Son and believes," verse 40.

But note the opposite, "all that the Father gives me," verse 37, and "all that He has given me," verse 39.

We will see more of this in the following passages, but He repeatedly promised to all He would "raise them up at the last day," verses 39, 40, 44, and 54. For as Jesus said, "I have come down from heaven not to do my will but to do the will of Him who sent me," verse 38. The Father's will is "not wanting anyone to perish, but everyone to come to repentance," 2 Peter 3:9

41–45   Jesus noted in Luke 4:24–27, that those closest to the prophets God sent were the last to recognize their message, and gave examples. Jesus experienced it from His own family, 7:5, and Mark 3:21.

In these verses in John, the Jews debated how He could be from heaven, when they knew of His earthly birth. Later, verse 62, Jesus asks how they would cope if they see Him ascend back into heaven? He referred here, of course, to His ascension.

Jesus again raised the apparent dilemma of obtaining salvation; both through the Father's call, or by personal choice. Note the constant use of both in this list.

> **The Father Draws.** 37, All the Father gives me; 39, All He has given me; 44, None can come unless the Father draws them; and 65, The Father enables him.
>
> **We Choose.** 35, He who comes and believes; 40, Everyone who looks to the Son and believes; 45, Everyone who listens and learns; and 47, He who believes.

Jesus' incorporation of both sides of this issue, seemingly at random, shows both ideas came naturally to Him. Both are true in God's plan. A story that illustrates this apparent dovetailing of opposite views pictures an archway into heaven. Over the front of the arch are the words, "Whosoever Will May Come." After passing through the arch, over the rear of the arch are the words, "Chosen from the Foundation of the World." Both are true!

Jesus quoted Isaiah 54:13, "They will all be taught by God." That chapter speaks of the restoration of Israel, and here Jesus widened it to mean the reconciliation of men and women to God. Those who "listen," "learn," and hear God's words will be the ones who come to Jesus, for they recognize Him.

46–51   Jesus claimed He was the only one who has seen God. It parallels 14: 9, "anyone who has seen me has seen the Father." At that event, Philip had not grasped Jesus was the Son who "is the radiance of God's glory and the exact representation of His being," Hebrews 1:3. Recognizing the Son's deity is the basis of belief that saves; no one else was worthy to procure salvation for us.

For the third time in this chapter Jesus emphasized a critical truth.

I tell you the truth, he who believes has everlasting life.

Jesus used the emphatic pronoun in proclaiming "I *am* the bread of life." He drew a parallel between the manna, which provided daily food, and Himself, the life-giving bread. Those who ate the manna still died. Jesus offered Himself as the living bread that gives eternal life.

Natural human life will run its course, but the life Jesus gives is a higher (spiritual) life that will live on into eternity. Recall Jesus' words in 11:25–26, "I *am* the resurrection and the life. He who believes in me will live, even though he dies; and whoever lives and believes in me will never die." Eternal life is available to us now!

Then Jesus opened up a fresh way of expressing this new life, by eating this bread, which is His flesh, given (sacrificed) for the world. In so doing, He anticipated His death on the cross, "This bread is my flesh, which I will give for the life of the world."

52–59   The Jews' response showed they were still stuck in earthly thinking. Despite this, Jesus doubled down using the expression to "eat His flesh" and "drink His blood," four times, stating it as a critical truth.

> I tell you the truth, unless you eat the flesh of the Son of
> Man and drink his blood, you have no life in you.

He refused to explain the meaning in spiritual terms, wanting them to make the connection. A hint was given in verses 49–51 and here again in verse 58: "This is the bread that came down from heaven. Your forefathers ate manna and died, but he who feeds on this bread will live forever."

This subject reminds us of the Passover, the forerunner of our communion. To avoid the destroying angel, the Hebrews were to eat the flesh of the lamb and paint the blood on the doorframe of the Hebrew home. In a similar way, accepting both His broken body and blood from the cross is necessary for our salvation.

It is also a reminder of communion, or the Lord's Table. Catholics believe the bread and wine actually change into the physical body and blood of Jesus. Protestants consider the bread and wine of symbols of His body and blood, which picture His death as our salvation.

The Division

60–66   In this passage, the "hangers on," those who sought only fulfillment of earthly needs, were separated from the true believers, those who recognized His offer of spiritual, eternal life.

This point marked the divergent ways of those who believed in Jesus and those who did not. What that belief entailed came later with Peters' confession. Others, beside the twelve, had followed Him to this time; note the seventy-two He sent out in Luke 10:1. Obviously, even among His followers, there were those who only had superficial or deficient belief in Jesus.

They were offended because of Him. Jesus always gives offence to those who wish to mold Him into their idea of God. Compare the Jewish leadership seeking signs and the Greeks—typical of current society—who seek for "wisdom." But Jesus

Christ crucified is "a stumbling block to Jews and foolishness to Gentiles," 1 Corinthians 1:23.

Jesus raised the question what their response might be if they saw Jesus rise back into heaven, Acts 1:9–11 probably still insufficient to convince those who would not believe. Compare Luke 16:31, "[Jesus] said to him, 'If they do not listen to Moses and the Prophets, they will not be convinced even if someone rises from the dead.'"

Jesus also tried to enlighten them once more, indicating He was talking of spiritual things, "The Spirit gives life; the flesh counts for nothing. The words I have spoken to you are Spirit and they are life," but His skeptical listeners were still not convinced and "turned back and no longer followed Him." Jesus knew who they would be for He knows His own, 10:14, "I am the good shepherd; I know my sheep and my sheep know me."

67–71   Jesus sought reassurance the twelve would not leave Him. Peter spoke for them all, "Lord, to whom shall we go? You have the words of eternal life. We believe and know that you are the Holy One of God." Yet Jesus knew that even among this apparently dedicated twelve was one who would betray Him.

7

The Persecution Intensifies

If anyone chooses to do God's will, he will find out whether my teaching comes from God or whether I speak on my own.
John 7:17

This chapter lays the groundwork for the increasing intensity of persecution against Jesus, as we travel through the remainder of John's gospel, that eventually ended in His crucifixion.

Jesus at the Feast of Tabernacles

1–5   Jesus stayed in Galilee because He knew the Jews in Jerusalem were seeking to take His life. He stayed away, not from fear, but as the next verses show, He knew His time "had not yet come."

Jesus' brothers challenged Him with mockery to go to the Feast of Tabernacles. They did not believe who He was and treated Him like some travelling snake oil salesman, telling Him to "become a public figure" to advance His miracle business.

6–9   Jesus' answer carried an important message, repeated frequently, that His time had not yet come, see 2:4, verses 6, 8, 30, and 8:20. It is also implied in verses 26, 44, and

45–46. While Jesus took reasonable precautions, the message was clear: no one could forestall the plan God had prepared.

Note Jesus' clear delineation of evil in verse 7. The Jews' enforced political correctness did not cow Him, even though they hated Him as a result. The establishment will not love Christians either if they stand for truth in any culture, including our own.

The important lesson for us is that our lives are in God's hands, and as we follow His purpose for us, nothing can interfere with the life God has planned for us, and that it will fulfill His purpose.

10–13   Eventually, Jesus did go to the Feast, a seven-day celebration of God's provision when the Hebrews were freed from Egypt. For this week of celebration, they lived in booths made of boughs and foliage. Jesus went in private, and heard the rumours about Him.

Those rumours were not hard to find, although any overt discussion would draw the wrath of the Jewish leadership. The idea that He was a "good man" would not fly, because of the outrageous claims Jesus made. Others took a more pragmatic approach: He was a deceiver, which was only appropriate if Jesus was lying about His status.

14–19   Jesus began to teach halfway through the feast. Perhaps He was incensed at the distortion of God's word, and despite the threat of assassination, felt compelled to preach the truth. We do not know what He taught in that 14th verse, but it was enough to astound the people.

Jesus' teaching was formidable for it was the truth. They pondered how He received this convincing education without formal training. His mastery, understanding, and insightful exposition of the Old Testament Scriptures was not only unmatched by the learned, but also carried authority, compare Matthew 7:29. Whereas the prophets said, "Thus says the Lord," Jesus said, "I tell you."

Jesus answered their question simply: His words came

directly from the Father who had sent Him, and He asserted that those who do God's will would learn the truth of His claim. Truth is eventually self-authenticating and a culture built on lies will finally collapse. Those who speak what they devise, are seeking their own fame, not God's honour.

Jesus accused His listeners of not keeping Moses' law, so they had no right to condemn another they supposed was wrong, "Why are you trying to kill me?" As He continued, it became clear the Jews accusation of Him was healing the lame man on the Sabbath, 5:16–18. He countered with their acceptance of circumcision on the eighth day, even if that was a Sabbath. So, He argued, it must also be right to make a man whole on the Sabbath; maintaining tradition does not always serve justice.

The Jews Argue Who Jesus Is

25–29   From here, the argument about Jesus swung back and forth. Why had the authorities not arrested Him if they were trying to kill Him? Did they think He was the Messiah? This led some in the crowd to think He might be. Others argued He could not be, because they knew His beginnings and, they assumed, no one would know Messiah's origin.

Jesus agreed they knew His earthly history, but He repeated and maintained in the clearest terms that He knew the one who sent Him because He came from the Father. Jesus later claimed they did not know the Father because they did not recognize Him, 8:19.

30–39   The controversy raged on. Some tried to seize Him. Others believed in Jesus for the miracles He performed. This prompted the Pharisees to send temple guards to arrest Him. But Jesus continued teaching. Adding to the idea the Jews did not know where He came from, He claimed they would not know where He was going either. Looking toward His eventual ascension, He said He would return to the One who sent Him; they would not find Him, nor could they follow Him.

61

This latest of Jesus sayings, as usual, bewildered them. If they could not conceive where He came from neither would they understand His disappearance. Jesus' response was to issue His invitation again to the crowd to believe and receive living water from Him, see Isaiah 55:1, Revelation 22:1, and recall the woman at the well, 4:10. In turn, that living water would flow from those who received it.

John clarified Jesus was speaking of the Holy Spirit whom believers in Him would receive upon His ascension back to glory, see 14:16–17, and Acts 1:8 and 2:1–4.

40–44   This further increased the confusion and misinformation among the Jews. Was Jesus the Prophet who was to come, or was He the Christ? But how could He be the Christ if He came from Galilee as they supposed, He should come from Bethlehem, Micah 5:2 and be David's descendent, Isaiah 9:7.

As usual, Jesus' teaching divided His listeners. Those who opposed Him tried to seize Him, "But no-one laid a hand upon Him."

45–53   The temple guards returned to the Jewish leaders without Jesus. The reason? "No one ever spoke the way this man does." The guards were as astonished at Jesus teaching as the crowd was. The authority with which He spoke countered the authority of those who sent them.

The Pharisees replied with scorn. They had not believed Him, and the mob who listened were ignorant and cursed. They could be characterized today as a basket of deplorables made famous by Hillary Clinton. But as Jesus said, "You have hidden these things from the wise and learned, and revealed them to little children," Matthew 11:25.

Nicodemus sought to defend Jesus, urging trial before condemning Him. The others seized on the rumour, whether they believed it or not, that Jesus came from Galilee. Therefore, His claims were sacrilege and He condemned Himself. The final sentence, "Then each went to his own home," suggests the Jews had settled the whole argument. Jesus was an imposter and His claims deserved the death penalty.

8

The Truth About Truth

I am the light of the world. Whoever follows me will never walk in darkness, but will have the light of life.

John 8:12

This chapter opens with Jesus proclaiming Himself the Light of the world, and repeatedly stating the ultimate truth by saying who He was, to the obtuse ignorance of most of the Jews. But in the ensuing exchange, Jesus makes His most damning statement against the Jewish leadership yet. Although they believed themselves to be God's children, He accuses them of adopting Satan as their father, for if they were God's children and knew Him as their Father, they would have recognized Jesus.

The Woman Taken in Adultery

1–6a This story is not included in the earliest manuscripts. Therefore, while we should take its authenticity advisedly, the content seems consistent with the wisdom with which Jesus dealt with other encounters. The early fathers also referenced it as early as A.D. 100.

After spending the night at the Mount of Olives, Jesus returned to the temple courts to teach. There the Jews had devised a plan to trap Jesus. To agree to stoning a woman taken in adultery would set Jesus against the Romans who retained the authority to administer the death penalty. However, to refuse to stone her set Jesus against the Jewish Law.

6b–11 What did Jesus write on the ground? We can only speculate, but Billy Graham once suggested it was the Ten Commandments. This would explain the Jews' slow departure as the law convicted them. Further, the law required trial of both the man and woman taken in adultery, and Jesus refused to be complicit in their deceit.

Although Jesus did not condemn her, neither did He condone her sin. His desire was not for judgment, but for transformation. During this period of grace, we need to be compassionate with those caught up in sin, because we are also sinners.

Jesus Affirms His Identity

12 During the light filled Feast of Tabernacles Jesus proclaimed, "I *am* the light of the world," using the emphatic form of "I am." Then as now, Jesus spoke into the spiritual darkness of humankind estranged from God. "Whoever follows me will never walk in darkness, but will have the light of life."

The creation story shows God as the author of natural light three days before the creation of the sun and moon, and John reminds us the Lord God and the Lamb are the complete source of light in the New Jerusalem, Revelation 21:23, and 22:5. But the New Testament most frequently uses light as a metaphor for truth, recall John's witness in 1:3–4, and the latter part of this chapter deals with the Jews continual denial of the truth of Jesus identity.

13–16 Two witnesses should, according to the law, confirm the issue of Jesus' identity. This was the Pharisees challenge in verse 13. The Jews refused to accept His heavenly origin. In fact, Jesus plainly stated they had no idea where He came from or where He would go, so they demanded proof by human standards.

Jesus answered in two parts. First, He confirmed His own witness was sufficient testimony to who He was, for He came from the source of all truth, the Father. Similarly, while a judge calls for witnesses, he does not require witnesses for himself.

But Jesus did not come the first time to judge but to save, although He already had authority from the Father to judge, 5:26–27. Thus, His future judgment will be just because "I stand with the Father, who sent me." Truth and justice go hand in hand.

17–20   Second, to satisfy their demands, and to draw out their questions, He conceded the law required two witnesses, and He offered Himself and the Father. This drew the expected retort, "where is your Father?" and opened the way for Jesus to proclaim His deity through the remainder of the chapter.

Jesus started with a claim that He repeated several times, and in various ways: "'You do not know me or my Father,' Jesus replied. 'If you knew me, you would know my Father also.'" This watershed statement undergirded the remainder of His teaching. The Jews understood what He said, it was clear blasphemy to them, but they could not seize Him, "for His time had not yet come."

21–30   Jesus extended His claim. Not only did they not know who He was, neither did they know where He was going, specifically adding it was where they could not go. He declared their sin prevented them going to where He would be going if they "do not believe that I *am* [the one I claim to be], you will indeed die in your sins." Again Jesus used the emphatic form of "I am."

They were baffled by the spiritual significance of His teaching. They wondered if He would kill himself! In frustration they asked, "Who are you?" Perhaps Jesus was irritated also, "Just what I have been claiming all along." Then He prepared them for more bad news.

"I have much to say in judgment of you. But He who sent me is reliable, and what I have heard from Him I tell the world." Judgment is inevitable without accepting Jesus.

They still did not believe Him, so He gave them a future proof: when they crucify Him (lifted up) then they will know He is the "I am," see Matthew 27:54. His resurrection and ascension will augment His claim. Jesus again emphasized that what He was doing pleased the Father who continued to be with Him. Some heard Him and placed their faith in Him.

Jesus Defines the Truth

31–41   To those who believed in Him, Jesus taught that following His teaching would confirm their faith, that is, action betrays belief. As the chapter unfolds, His teaching clearly stretched some beyond credulity; His teaching was not only the primary truth, but also the ultimate source of freedom, as He states a vital truth: "You will know the truth, and the truth will set you free."

The Jews claimed Abraham as their father, and so claimed they were free and not slaves. Jesus countered with a critical truth that sin is the source of bondage, from which no earthly father could free them.

> I tell you the truth, everyone who sins is a slave to sin.
> Now a slave has no permanent place in the family, but
> a son belongs to it forever.

Jesus came to make them sons, and as the Son Himself, He could provide freedom from both the penalty and power of sin. But that depended on believing the truth of who He was.

Jesus now carefully explained that although the Jews were Abraham's physical descendants, Abraham was not their father. Abraham would not kill the one sent from above, which they were trying to do, proving their father was someone else. Jesus contrasted what He witnessed from the Father, against what they heard from their father—a different father! The

Jews answer was to raise the stakes, claiming God as their Father.

42–47   Jesus declared, "If God were your Father, you would love me, for I came from God," and continued His explanation. Then He asks the rhetorical question: "Why is my language not clear to you?" Today, we would say, "What part don't you understand?"

The answer may surprise us, but it enraged the Jews. At this point, Jesus unambiguously stated their father was the devil who was both a murderer and a liar. Jesus turned the hypocrisy of the Jews on its head; nothing else could have made Jesus their greatest enemy.

Proof they believed Satan's lies was their obsession on murdering Jesus Himself. The devil foments discord and destruction through all who believe in his lies. In fact, as Jesus said, "he was a murderer from the beginning." Recall Cain and Abel, and the monstrous human loss by violence throughout history.

The separation that Jesus set out here is both radical and comprehensive. The only truth comes through Jesus Christ: "Grace and truth came through Jesus Christ," 1:17, who is the truth, 14:6. Those who belong to God recognize and believe Him. Those who ignore or reject Him, knowingly or unknowingly, are fulfilling Satan's objectives.

48–59   The Jews only answer was to accuse Jesus of being a Samaritan (a derisive term for blasphemers), or just plain crazy (demon-possessed). In dishonoring Jesus, the Jews dishonored God, whereas God glorified Jesus; compare His baptism, Matthew 3:16-17.

Then Jesus added another critical truth that further enraged them.

I tell you the truth, if anyone keeps my word, he will never see death.

Was Jesus greater that Abraham who died along with all the prophets? The final insult followed: "Who do you think you are?" a typical taunt of rejection.

Jesus' defense was simply His adherence to the truth. The Father was the one who glorified Jesus, and Jesus spoke the truth, not lies like His hearers. Even Abraham rejoiced to know Jesus' appearance: "He saw it and was glad." Three times, God told Abraham that all peoples on earth would be blessed through his offspring, Genesis 12:3, 18:18, and 22:18. And that offspring was Jesus.

In answer to their disbelief that Jesus had seen Abraham, Jesus answered with the unforgettable and critical truth and His repeated emphatic use of "I am,"

I tell you the truth . . . before Abraham was born, I am!

By mixing the tenses, Jesus affirmed He was in the present before Abraham was born. The Jews totally revered the name "I am" as the name of God given to Moses in Exodus 3:13–15. Jesus was declaring Himself to be that "I am."

For the Jews, this was the ultimate blasphemy, and it was more than the Jews could stand. The mob tried to stone Him, but again He slipped away from them. Jesus was the outcast throughout His ministry, with few believing in Him, the majority eventually wanting Him crucified. Christians can expect no less rejection from the cultures in which they live.

9

Jesus Heals the Man Born Blind

"One thing I do know. I was blind but now I see!"

John 9:25

This chapter is a delightful story of a man blind from birth, healed by Jesus, and this man's subsequent rejection by the Jewish leadership. It is a story of simple faith over entrenched legalism.

The Man is Healed

1–5   To the disciples, the blind man was just a curiosity as they trotted out the traditional dogma that he or his parents had sinned to produce his blindness. Jesus responded his blindness had nothing to do with personal or family sin. Nor should we assume God blinded the man for His glory.

Adversity may attach to personal sin. As my mother used to say, "Feet in the puddles means cold in the head." But society's sin touches us all. Consider a drunk driver maiming a pedestrian. God can manifest His glory against the effects of sin to any person at any time.

In verse 5 He claimed, "*I am* the light of the world." This is one of the many "I am" sayings of Jesus already noted in chapters 4, 6, 7, and 8, and which will occur again subsequent chapters. In all of these, as here, Jesus used the emphatic pronoun, continually referring Himself to the great "I am" of Exodus 3:14.

Some suggest the coming night in verse 4, commenced when Jesus left planet earth. But God has continued to work since Jesus' ascension, the light mediated by others who themselves become the light of the world, see Matthew 5:14. Jesus may also have referred to the darkness of persecution after His ascension that will attempt to stifle His servants' work.

Furthermore, light is a symbol of truth and understanding. While Jesus caused natural light to pierce this man's eyes, He also brought an understanding by which the man confounded even the Jewish leadership.

6–12   The man's actual healing is only a small part of the story covering only two verses. However, do not be fooled by its minor reference here. This was an astounding miracle, not of restored sight, but of newly created sight to a man whose blindness was congenital.

While it may have been the greatest thing in the man's life, the remainder of the chapter deals with the fallout. Predominantly, did the miracle really happen? Already, people who had known the man were questioning his recovery. Some said, "He only looks like him," while others confirmed it was him.

No amount of evidence will convince those who do not *want* to see. But the man himself knew what had happened and forthrightly proclaimed it to all who questioned him. Note his simple repeat of Jesus' procedure to both the local doubters and later to the Pharisees.

The Pharisees Investigate

13–16   As it often happened, Jesus healed on the Sabbath. The Pharisees believed this broke the law and so disproved Jesus' heavenly origin. The man responded to the Pharisees with a simple statement of the truth: "He put mud on my eyes . . . and I washed and now I see."

The Pharisees could not debate the man's experience, only believe it or not, and the man's story split the Pharisees. Experience is a powerful weapon as witness to Christ's work whether believed or not. It is not open to debate like a claim of personal belief.

17–23   The Pharisees only way out was to discredit the man and so ignore his story. So they asked who the man thought Jesus was. Acknowledging Jesus as the Christ or Messiah would result in excommunication. The man's response, probably a guess, "He is a prophet," was a safe answer. But he, like the woman at the well, certainly saw Jesus as a man of God.

The Pharisees did not believe the man's story. To believe him would complicate their beliefs. Perhaps his parents would provide a way out. This seemed most likely, as they were afraid of the Pharisees. They admitted he was their son born blind and could now see, but refused to get embroiled in a debate that could put them out of the synagogue.

24–27   So the Pharisees questioned the man again. Under the solemn charge, "Give glory to God," they asked him if he considered Jesus a sinner. Both "yes" and "no" created a problem. If he agreed Jesus was a sinner he denied his healing, for in the Jews' view, sinners cannot do miracles. If he said Jesus was not a sinner, he risked dismissal from the synagogue.

So he just stuck to his story, "I was blind but now I see." All who recognize Jesus as Saviour can repeat these words, released from spiritual blindness.

Again, the Pharisees could not debate his testimony. So they again asked the man how he was healed. Now the man's feisty spirit showed up; he did not need to repeat his story. Were they interested in following Jesus? He taunted them, "Do you want to become His disciples too?"

73

28–34   Now a battle of wits began between the Pharisees the man healed from blindness. Note the response of the Pharisees when they had no answer for the man: insults and defamation. A typical response by those whose beliefs are shown to be indefensible is to pull rank, hurl abuse, or verbally or physically attack, those who oppose them.

Now the man destroyed the Pharisees' position. Surely, he argued, this man must come from God because first, He "opened my eyes." Second, "[God] only listens to the godly man who does His will," and third, if this Jesus "were not from God, He could do nothing."

Again, the Pharisees could only pull rank. They said he was a sinner from birth, implying they were not! He was not fit to lecture them, and without valid evidence, they threw him out of the synagogue.

Jesus Restores the Man

31–38   Jesus found the man searching for Him because the Pharisees threw him out. Jesus asked him if he believed in the Messiah–the Son of Man. Despite his spirited defense against the Pharisees, the man was still confused about Jesus. He wanted to believe but needed to know who Jesus was. Jesus confirmed He was the Son of Man predicted in Daniel, and the man believed.

Note Jesus' compassion for the abused man, a symptom of His compassion for the oppressed. To find answers to confusion, first requires belief in Him. Anselm of Canterbury claimed: "I *believe* so that I may *understand*." The man believed, then worshiped Jesus. Recall that only God can be worshiped, and by receiving worship, Jesus implicitly confirmed His deity.

39–41   Finally, Jesus applied the man's healing to His mission. He came "into this world, so that the blind will see and those who see will become blind." While we can realize

He came to heal the blind, His claim to blind those who see is more difficult.

His words referred of course to the Pharisees. Those who claim to see, but refuse to recognize Jesus, are "guilty of sin," because their blindness is a choice, see Isaiah 6:9–10, quoted by Jesus in Matthew 13:13–15. Today's Pharisees, like those of Jesus' day, are those who reject Jesus' authority because He does not fit into their personally predetermined beliefs.

10

The Good Shepherd

I am the Good Shepherd.
The Good Shepherd lays down His life for the sheep

John 10:11

The background for this chapter is Ezekiel chapter 34, in which the Lord accuses the shepherds of God's people of abusing and plundering the sheep. See God's complaint against them in Ezekiel 34:1–4, but also read the promise of one shepherd, David, to care for them, in the later verses of this chapter, 23–24. Jesus, with the right to David's throne, claimed to be that Shepherd.

Not only does Jesus have authority from God to claim this, but as the chapter unfolds, He is the only one who cares for God's people; those who claim entry into God's Kingdom by some other means are "thieves and robbers," more concerned with their own welfare than for God's people.

The Good Shepherd Cares for His Flock

1–5 Note the context from chapter 9. The good shepherd cares for the sheep, the others are thieves and robbers. Jesus cared for the man born blind; the Pharisees did not. Those listening would have realized Jesus was comparing the Pharisees with thieves and robbers, and Himself with the Good Shepherd.

Twice in this chapter, Jesus declares a critical truth, commencing at verse 1.

> *I tell you the truth, the man who does not enter the*
> *sheep pen by the gate, but climbs in by some other way,*
> *is a thief and a robber.*

He emphasized there is only one way into the Kingdom of God: through Him; compare 14:6.

The gatekeeper of the sheepfold, which might hold several flocks, would let only the legitimate shepherds into the fold who cared for the sheep. Each shepherd called his small flock by name, and they recognized the shepherd's voice. They would follow only him.

Eastern shepherds led their sheep; they did not drive them. Out of the fold, the sheep would follow him, knowing he would protect and feed them, search for and heal the lost and injured. They would run from a voice they did not know.

6–8   The disciples understood the everyday description of shepherding life, but could not figure why Jesus told them what they already knew. So Jesus tried to give them greater insight, calling Himself the gate keeper as a critical truth.

> *I tell you the truth*, I am *the gate for the sheep.*

His words, "*I am* the Gate," used the emphatic form for "I am" the Jews would recognize as the name God gave Himself in Exodus 3:14–15.

As the Gate, Jesus is the protector of all who come into His fold. As he says in verse 28, "No-one can snatch them out of my hand." Those who came before Him were not interested in the welfare of the flock, but were like the shepherds of Ezekiel 34, and the Pharisees and chief priests who abused and exploited those committed to their care.

9–10   Jesus again used the emphatic version of "I *am* the Gate." In these verses, He contrasted His care for the sheep against the abuse of others. As the gatekeeper, He regulated the coming and going of the shepherds who ensured the sheep find good pasture. In doing so, He made sure they had a full life. Note the idea of under-shepherds, also from Ezekiel 34, who care for the small flocks.

11–13 Jesus changed the metaphor in this verse, again using the emphatic pronoun as He introduced a different role: "I *am* the Good Shepherd." Calling Himself the Good Shepherd reminded the listening Jews that the "Lord is my shepherd," Psalm 23:1. Elsewhere, God is known as the Shepherd of Israel, Psalm 80:1, Isaiah 40:10–11, as well as Ezekiel 34.

Then Jesus opened a theme that will run through to verse 18, "The Good Shepherd lays down His life for the sheep." This is in contrast to the hired man, who cares for his status and wages more than the welfare of the sheep. Again, He referenced the Jewish leadership who were more concerned with their reputation than those in their care. Recall Jesus' words, still relevant today, "Watch out for false prophets. They come to you in sheep's clothing, but inwardly they are ferocious wolves," Matthew 7:15. There, Jesus advised, see how they live, in order to discern them. They are strangers' voices.

14–16 Again Jesus repeated, with the same emphasis: "I *am* the Good Shepherd." He referred back to the opening verses of this chapter, as He explained to His perplexed disciples He knows His sheep and they know Him. Note the comparison: Jesus and His sheep know each other as He and the Father know each other. It is that knowledge that keeps His sheep safe because they recognize His voice and follow only Him.

Those listening, and accepting Jesus, might assume He came for His people, the Jews. But other sheep, most probably the Gentiles, would also become part of the one flock under one shepherd, Jesus.

17–21 In these verses, note the reason God loves the Son. He lays down His life; He was willing to sacrifice Himself for God's people.

Then Jesus made the most amazing claim: He had complete control over His death and return to life again. That claim is one that belongs only to God, "The Lord brings death and makes alive; He brings down to the grave and raises up," 1 Samuel 2:6. As the Son of God, Jesus received the same authority.

As usual, Jesus' claims divided His hearers, compare 7:43, 9:16. Some, without thought, just assumed Him a lunatic—demon possessed—for the claims He made. For others, that did not make sense; demons do not open blind eyes!

The Jews' Disbelief

22–25   It was Hanukkah, the feast remembering the dedication of the temple by Judas Maccabeus, after being profaned by Antiochus Epiphanes two hundred years earlier. As Jesus walked in Solomon's colonnade, the Jews continually asked if He was the Christ (or Messiah). They were probably the Jewish leadership bent on accusing Jesus. Jesus answered that He had already told them.

Recall Jesus had confirmed His identity to the woman at the well, 4:25–26, and the blind man He had healed, 9:35–37. The Jews had understood His earlier comments, 5:18, and His enigmatic phrase, "before Abraham was born, I am!" 8:58. They understood His claim to be God, and tried to stone Him on both occasions. Note also, His claim of authority to Judge in 5:27–30, also God's prerogative.

In addition, His miracles spoke for His identity. Those miracles were works the Father had given Him to do, and His words and His works were consistent.

26–33   Jesus returned to the importance of recognition. As before, He pointed out they did not believe because they were not His sheep. His sheep, as we learned, recognize His voice, they inherit eternal life and are secure in Him forever. Jesus again claimed He and the Father are one; no one can snatch those the Father has given Jesus from His hand, nor from the Father's hand, for He "is greater than all."

So the Jews attempted to stone Him again. Their reason? "For blasphemy, because you, a mere man, claim to be God." They recognized what He said; they just did not believe Him. Why? Jesus was blunt: "You do not believe because you are not my sheep," verse 25.

34–39   This is a poorly understood section. Jesus referred to Psalm 82 where the wicked judges and rulers of Israel had a godlike commission. But as Psalm 82:6–7 shows, "I said, 'You are "gods"; you are all sons of the Most High.' But you will die like mere men; you will fall like every other ruler." Jesus argued that if *they* were called gods, how much more the One sent from the Father.

Jesus gave them two options for belief: first believe Him if He did the Father's will, or second, believe His miracles were from God. Both these showed Jesus and the Father were one. They refused to believe Him and again tried to seize Him, but He evaded them.

40–42   Jesus left Jerusalem and crossed the Jordan. During His time there, many believed on Him because, they said, "All that John [the Baptist] said about this man was true."

11

Lazarus is Raised from the Dead

"I am the resurrection and the life. He who believes in me will live, even though he dies; and whoever lives and believes in me will never die."

John 11:25-26

This is a long chapter, but mostly narrative, and an easier read than previous chapters. Chapters 9 through 12 all take place the few weeks before the Passover when Jesus was crucified. References back to the healed blind man in chapters 10 and 11, and the reference back to Lazarus in chapter 12, confirm a series of events over a short period.

The Death of Lazarus

1-3 John introduces the family of Martha, Mary and Lazarus in these verses, noting they were brother and sisters. Lazarus had fallen sick and Mary was the one in 12:3 who washed Jesus' feet with her hair. Do not confuse her with the unnamed woman who performed a similar ritual in Luke 7:37–38.

4-6 Jesus' delay before going to the family He loved, sheds some light on apparent unanswered prayer. While there are other reasons we could deduce from Scripture, His delay was not for lack of love for the family. This instance, and the man born blind of chapter 9, gives one reason for delay: God's glory would be revealed in each instance. It's too easy in dire circumstances to seek a resolution for our own comfort, when, as His followers, it is God's glory we seek; that He will accomplish His work, often through our adversity.

Jesus' claim that Lazarus' sickness would not end in death appears to contradict the story; Lazarus did die! But in fact, the final resolution did not end in death, because Jesus raised Lazarus.

7–10 Recall that Jesus had departed Jerusalem after another altercation with the Jews in which they tried to kill Him, 10:33. As He had indicated many times earlier, His time "had not yet come," but He still took precautions that avoided testing God. Satan's claim that angels would save Jesus if He jumped off the temple, Matthew 4:5–7, was probably true, Psalm 91:11–12, but Jesus would not put God to the test. He came to do the Father's will, and showmanship was not part of it.

However, this occasion was different. When the disciples tried to dissuade Him, He responded with the enigmatic answer in verse 10. The natural knowledge that it is easier to walk in daylight than at night, was meant as a symbol that we must walk in God's light when called to do so. Recall His previous comment to work while we have the light in 9:4. The time for His final sacrifice was near, and He set out resolutely to face it, Isaiah 50:4–9, note verse 7. This was "His time!"

11–16 It is doubtful the disciples understood Jesus' answer in verses 9 and 10, just as they did not understand Jesus' use of sleep for Lazarus' death. As Jesus explained Lazarus was dead, He also declared His delay was "so that you may believe." God's glory would be shown in a way that would encourage their belief and convince others.

Thomas, his doubting streak considering Jesus' return to Judea foolish, resigned himself to die with Jesus. However, his doubt did not turn into unbelief; he was still committed to Jesus. Doubt is not sin, but is the temptation not to believe.

17–19   The journey to Bethany was some distance, and by the time Jesus arrived there, Lazarus had been dead four days, so any raising of Lazarus from death could not be disputed. As Bethany was close to Jerusalem, many Jews from there had come to grieve with Martha and Mary, so news of any miracle would spread quickly. With the Jews out to kill Him, this was not a good time to be close to Jerusalem, but Jesus' time was close, see 12:23. This raising of Lazarus would be the last sign of Jesus' identity before His crucifixion.

20–27   Martha went to meet Jesus. The exchanges between Jesus and Martha provide us with a legacy of understanding about life and death. Martha first conveyed her belief in Jesus' healing ability, "If you had been here, my brother would not have died."

But she went on to explore another possibility, "even now God will give you whatever you ask." Was it possible He could raise the dead? Jesus' response did not seem forthcoming: "Your brother will rise again." Was that now or later? Martha hedged behind the common wisdom, "I know he will rise again in the resurrection at the last day."

In response, Jesus set out a basic truth using the emphatic pronoun, "I *am* the resurrection and the life. He who believes in me will live, even though he dies; and whoever lives and believes in me will never die." He had claimed power over life and death shortly before, 10:17–18, and here He claims the same.

However, His power over death was not for Him alone. All who believe in Him "will live, even though he dies." Jesus acknowledged physical death, after all, Lazarus had died. But bodily death was not the end, life continued, "Whoever lives and believes in me will never die."

When asked if she believed that, Martha not only confirmed her belief in a future life, but also proclaimed, "I believe that

85

you are the Christ, the Son of God, who was to come into the world." Jesus led her to the point where she made the public confession of her faith in Jesus Christ, her expected Messiah. Recall 3:16.

28–37   For some reason, Jesus stayed for a while at the place where He met Martha. Perhaps the grave was closer to this point than Mary and Martha's house, as verses 31 and 34 may suggest. It was here that Mary came to meet Jesus with the same allegation as Martha: "Lord, if you had been here, my brother would not have died." But in her grief, she didn't follow up with the statements of faith Martha had expressed.

Seeing her weeping with her friends, Jesus was moved and troubled, or better, emotionally stirred up inside. Jesus wept, reminding us, "we do not have a high priest who is unable to sympathize with our weaknesses," Hebrews 4:15. It was time to bring this distress to a halt, and He followed the mourners to Lazarus' grave.

However, as always, skeptics questioned Jesus' actions. "Could not He who opened the eyes of the blind man have kept this man from dying?" They recalled Jesus' healing of the blind man, and accused Jesus of negligence toward those He loved.

Jesus Raises Lazarus

38–44   But Jesus' sorrow continued as He approached Lazarus' tomb. The tomb was similar to the one in which Jesus was later buried: a cave with a stone closing the entrance. When Jesus requested the stone removed, Martha, practical as ever, complained of the stench that would arise after four days dead. But the glory of God about to be displayed would dispense with that as Lazarus came out completely healed and alive.

Once the stone was removed, Jesus prayed to the Father aloud. His prayer was as much for His hearers as to God, so they would understand Jesus was sent from the Father. After calling with a loud voice, "Lazarus, come out," Lazarus appeared in his grave clothes. Jesus commanded he be released and let go. This was the final sign John records to authenticate Jesus' identity and authority before His crucifixion.

Recall also others who came out of their graves at Jesus' life-giving death, Matthew 27:52–53.

45–52 As we have seen in previous chapters, Jesus' words and actions always divided those observing Him. Some believed, but others hastened to tell the Pharisees of this miracle. The Jewish Leaders had hounded Jesus for much of His ministry, vainly trying to end it. But this major miracle, the talk of Jerusalem, brought them to action and they convened a meeting to deal with this troublemaker.

Their concern had nothing to do with their religion, but that Jesus might disrupt the delicate relationship they had with the occupying Roman authorities. Caiaphas, the high priest had a solution, what he considered the lesser of two evils; this man, Jesus, should be sacrificed for the good of the nation of Israel. His words were prophetic—God uses even those who oppose Him—for Jesus did die to bring salvation to the Jews.

However, John knowing of the worldwide ministry Jesus was promoting, added that other "children of God," beyond Israel, would enter God's Kingdom. Recall other sheep Jesus had, 10:16, and John's words about Jesus: "Look, the Lamb of God, who takes away the sin of *the world!*" my emphasis, 1:29.

53–57 Once the Sanhedrin had decided to kill Him, Jesus stayed away from Jerusalem. But as Passover approached, many were looking for Jesus, for the chief priests and Pharisees sought any information on Jesus' whereabouts so they might arrest Him.

12

Mary's Worship and the Jews' Unbelief

**I have come into the world as a light,
so that no one who believes in me should stay in darkness.**
John 12:46

Chapter 12 is another long chapter, some narrative and some teaching by Jesus. But His words were still profound and far reaching. The chapter easily divides into the worship of Jesus by Mary and the final entry of Jesus into Jerusalem as He faced crucifixion.

Mary Anoints Jesus

1–3   As this chapter opens, Jesus began His perilous journey to the cross. He arrived at Mary and Martha's house a few days before the Passover at which He would be crucified. It was during a dinner—cooked as usual by Martha—that Mary's anointing of Jesus took place. Recall that Jesus is the Messiah, or Christ, both meaning "the anointed one."

This anointing was an act of sacrificial worship, probably a year of accumulated savings poured over Jesus' feet. Her worship and love spread fragrance through the whole house.

4–8   But Mary's act was also prophetic, symbolizing the anointing of Jesus for His redeeming death. Recall the initial

89

anointing of Jesus for His ministry and sacrificial death was by the Holy Spirit, 1:32 and Luke 4:18-19. When Judas Iscariot accused Jesus that the money could have been used for the poor, Jesus upheld Mary's action as one that was intended to portray His coming burial.

It is difficult to think of Judas' action as anything but a lack of belief in Jesus' identity. As we see in his later betrayal of Jesus, it was clear that his reason for being a disciple was for the benefits he might gain. In this, he was no different from those that hailed Jesus' entry into Jerusalem, but eventually wanted Him crucified.

Jesus' comment, that the poor would always be with them, was not meant to convey that the poor were unimportant. But as Jesus said on another occasion, "Render unto God what is God's and to Caesar what is Caesar's." We need to recognize that there is a time and place for our giving to legitimate causes and needs, and also giving to God what is rightly His.

9–11   The raising of Lazarus from the dead was creating greater problems for the chief priests. John recounts Jews were going over to Jesus and putting their faith in Him as awareness of the raising of Lazarus grew. Now not only Jesus, but Lazarus also was in the crosshairs of the Jewish leadership. If they could kill Lazarus, then stories of Jesus raising the dead could be disputed in the future as mass hysteria.

Jesus' Triumphal Entry into Jerusalem

12–15   Those in Bethany sent word Jesus was on His way to Jerusalem, and many decided to welcome this great miracle worker—or was He a King?—into Jerusalem. Certainly, they appeared to recognize Jesus as coming "in the name of the Lord" and calling Him "the King of Israel."

Jesus entry into Jerusalem was decidedly low-key. Any real king entering the city would come with pomp, majesty, and a great retinue. Jesus, in keeping with His servant role during His first advent, came riding a donkey.

16–19   It was only later that the disciples realized they had been involved in fulfilling prophecy from Zechariah 9:9, "Rejoice greatly, O Daughter of Zion! Shout, Daughter of Jerusalem. See your King comes to you, righteous and having salvation, gentle and riding on a donkey, on a colt, the foal of a donkey."

That triumphal entry into Jerusalem was a pre-figuring of the day when He would come in to Jerusalem as King of all the earth and take up His rightful place as a Ruler of all. The news began to spread about Jesus, the miracle worker and the crowds had gone out to meet Him. That added to the frustration of the Pharisees, "Look how the whole world has gone after Him!"

Jesus Predicts His Death

20-26   Some outside the Jewish race, also attended the feast. They are called Greeks in the passage, but were probably more likely "God-fearers"—those who followed the Jewish faith but were reticent about circumcision. They were also interested in finding out about Jesus. His answer to their inquiry was very specific as Jesus introduced another critical truth:

> I tell you the truth, unless a kernel of wheat falls to the ground and dies, it remains only a single seed. But if it dies, it produces many seeds.

The reference to a seed of wheat dying in the ground certainly referred to Jesus, but as verse 25 suggests, it would also refer to those who would follow Him.

Jesus frequently mentioned the idea of losing yet gaining one's life. For instance, "Whoever finds his life will lose it, and whoever loses his life for my sake will find it," Matthew 10:39, compare Matthew 16:26. So Jesus repeated here, "The man who loves his life will lose it, while the man who hates his life in this world will keep it for eternal life."

This would apply to all, Jews and Greeks. Seeing Him meant following Him, for His servants would be with Him and God would honour them.

27-33   Now Jesus revealed His own anxiety for the future. Could He ask God to save Him from the hour that has come upon Him? Certainly not. "It was for this very reason I came to this hour." Then at Jesus' request that God's name be glorified, God answered from heaven with a thunderous voice, "I have glorified it, and will glorify it again."

Those with Jesus at the time heard it. As before at the raising of Lazarus, Jesus declared this voice was for the benefit of those around Him. Then Jesus triumphantly stated, "Now is the time for judgment on this world; now the prince of this world will be driven out." That same crucifixion at which Jesus defeated Satan, would draw all men to Himself. Clearly, not all people would be drawn to believe in Him, but everyone will have to face Jesus Christ to account for their belief or unbelief in Him.

34-36   The crowd raised the Jewish expectation that the Messiah would live forever. They also repeated the designation Jesus had used about Himself in verse 23, Son of Man, taken from Daniel 7:13-14. Notably, Jesus used this description of Himself some eighty times in the gospels, thirty times in John alone. So the question arose, how could Jesus claim to be the Messiah and live forever if He was to be crucified?

As we have noted previously, Jesus closely identified with the light. Jesus said to the Jews, that He would be with them for a short time longer, and they needed to believe in the light before He left and darkness enveloped them. There is no light or meaning for life without Jesus Christ. Then Jesus hid Himself. Jesus is always hidden from those who refuse to believe, and they remain in darkness. Jesus Christ, who is the truth, brings light to darkened hearts and minds.

The Jews' Unbelief

37-41   Jesus then taught on the reasons for unbelief. In doing so He referred back to Isaiah 53:1. There, even Isaiah wondered who might believe the story of a sacrificial God. That revelation several hundred years before Christ must have seemed as strange to the Jews then as the message Christ Himself was now bringing. Jesus went on to show why the Jews continued in unbelief "even after Jesus had done all these miraculous signs in their presence."

To explain, Jesus took up Isaiah's argument from Isaiah 6:9–10, found in Matthew chapter 13, to answer the question why He spoke in parables. In essence, the knowledge of the Kingdom of Heaven will only reach those with an open heart: "Whoever has will be given more, and he will have an abundance. Whoever does not have, even what he has will be taken from him," Matthew 13:12.

God acknowledges the choice of unbelief by hardening the heart. Recall Pharaoh who hardened his heart, and how God subsequently hardened Pharaoh's heart. Isaiah understood this "because he saw Jesus' glory and spoke about Him." The glory of God, which Isaiah saw in Isaiah 6, was also the glory of Christ.

42-46   Jesus was uncomplimentary about believers who remained in secret for fear of losing status. But as we noted with Lazarus, there were real dangers in believing in Jesus. Nicodemus confessed his belief in secret but remained in a place where he could intercede for Jesus, recall 7:50-52.

Jesus confirmed His identity by indicating that believing in Him meant believing in God. Seeing Jesus also meant seeing God, compare 14:9. As with many earlier pronouncements, the claim of deity–being equal with God–comes through clearly. The threat of arrest and death did not deter Him from proclaiming the truth. Truth is light, and as God is the source of light; believing in Him means leaving the darkness behind.

47-50   Jesus claimed He did not come to judge. Remember His words, "God did not send His Son into the world to condemn the world, but to save the world through Him," 3:17. Jesus Christ confirmed He will eventually be the judge in 5:26-27, but Jesus pointed out here that His words spoken during His earthly life would be the basis of judgment. This is true because He only spoke the words the Father had given Him. Judgment at the last day would be based on rejection of the words Jesus spoke at the Father's command. But for those who believe, His words are eternal life.

13

Jesus Washes the Disciples Feet, and Predicts His betrayal

"A new command I give you: Love one another.
As I have loved you, so you must love one another."
John 13:34

This chapter begins what is known as the Upper Room Discourse. Up to now, Jesus has generally been speaking to the general population, with little apparent result. But in chapters 13 to 17, He draws His disciples into a deeper understanding of the faith. This chapter records two incidents: the washing of the disciples' feet, and Jesus' prediction of His betrayal by Judas Iscariot.

Jesus Washes the Disciples' Feet.

1–5   Jesus' time had come; recall the many times He stated His time had not yet come, 7:6, 8, 30, and 8:20 and other references. Now He needed to prepare His disciples for His death and eventual departure. But throughout this passage, Jesus was keenly aware of His betrayer. Already, Satan was prompting Judas to betray Him. But Jesus was keenly aware of His identity and the responsibility that identity carried. He "knew that the Father had put all things under His power, and that He had come from God and was returning to God." Yet even that status did not deter Him

95

from expressing in physical terms the servant-hood nature of the faith.

So Jesus' first, and we assume most important lesson, was that of servant-hood. But washing their feet was not just teaching, He was expressing His love for His own. Love is expressed in service. Jesus washing the disciples' feet is reminiscent of Mary's act of love and devotion in the previous chapter, 12:3. In fact, the greatest joy is found in fulfilling Jesus' commands. Happiness is a byproduct of service. That is why David said, "surely goodness and love will follow me all the days of my life," Psalm 23:6, rather like a puppy dog's tail.

John notes that even as Jesus prepared to wash the disciple's feet, He knew Judas would betray Him, yet we assume that He washed Judas' feet with the others. Remember, washing feet was a necessary act of service by the host for his guests. Dusty roads and open sandals meant dirty feet. We take our shoes off when we visit another's house; eastern hosts washed their visitor's feet.

Jesus had already warned the disciples of their role as servants. When the mother of James and John asked for special status for her sons, Jesus pointed out that status depended on service, "Just as the Son of Man did not come to be served, but to serve, and to give His life as a ransom for many," Matthew 20:28. Thus Jesus went through the servant routine of washing the disciples' feet as an example of His future disciples' role.

Jesus graphically portrayed what Paul expressed in Philippians 2:6-8, Jesus "taking the very nature of a servant, being made in human likeness." As one commentator put it, "The form of God was not *exchanged for* the form of a servant; it was *revealed in* the form of a servant." It was a declaration of the character of God.

6–11   Peter did not want Jesus to wash his feet. His impulsiveness may have been misplaced, but he clearly saw his place as Christ's servant and not the other way around. Jesus told Peter that washing his feet was necessary. Peter would not understand the significance of it until later; it was a symbol of the cleansing that only comes from Jesus Christ.

At least Peter finally realized that he needed a complete washing, but Jesus comforted Peter, telling him he was clean. Belief in Jesus provides cleansing, because as Jesus said later, "You are already clean because of the word I have spoken to you," 15:3. Our salvation and cleansing is already complete in Christ, but daily confession and cleansing from walking the dusty road of life is also necessary.

However, constantly in Jesus' mind was the one who would betray Him; that one, who had his feet washed and dined with Jesus, had already rejected Jesus in his mind. Rejection of Jesus leaves us in our sin.

12–17   Jesus took time to explain to the disciples what He had done. They rightly called Him teacher and Lord, and Jesus accepted both titles, but the "Lord" had served them; a picture of the servant role they should be to each other. At this point Jesus introduced a critical truth.

> I tell you the truth, no servant is greater than his master, nor is a messenger greater than the one who sent him.

They should do no less for others than Jesus had done for them. Servant-hood was the mark of their ministry as it was of Jesus.

Recall Jesus words, "Not everyone who says to me, 'Lord, Lord,' will enter the Kingdom of Heaven, but only he who does the will of my Father who is in heaven," Matthew 7:21. Jesus followed this with the parable of the men who built their houses on the sand and the rock. It was the one "who hears these words of mine and *puts them into practice* is like a wise man who built his house on the rock," Matthew 7:24, my emphasis.

But they were not just to serve each other, they were to serve their wider sphere of influence as they matured in the faith. Obviously, that applies to all those who follow Jesus, and at times it may involve getting down and dirty to serve the neediest.

Jesus Predicts His Betrayal.

18–20   Any group aiming for reform is likely to have a spy from the opposition. Jesus knew of the betrayer among the twelve. Although He had sought them all to follow Him, Judas, though called, was not chosen. His anticipated rejection of Jesus was part of the plan for our redemption by Jesus' death: "The Son of Man will go as it has been decreed, but woe to that man who betrays Him," Luke 22:22.

Jesus recalled David's experience. One close to David had deceived him, Psalm 41:9. Jesus saw that as a prefiguring of His experience with Judas then being fulfilled. But even Judas' betrayal of Jesus would work towards the other disciples' belief. As Jesus' prediction came to pass before their eyes, they would have greater understanding that "I *am* He."

Here Jesus affirmed His deity, again using the emphatic "I *am*." He predicted the disciples would recognize who He is as the events of the next few days unfolded. He was, and still is, both the "I am" of Exodus 3:13–14, as well as the Son of Man of Daniel 7:14. All nations will eventually worship Him, as He brings peace and justice to the earth.

Jesus stressed this with a further critical truth,

> I tell you the truth, whoever accepts anyone I send accepts me; and whoever accepts me accepts the One who sent me.

Their acceptance, belief in Him, had further results. Those who accepted Jesus also accepted the Father who sent Him. But, in addition, those who accepted the truth from His disciples also accepted Jesus and the Father who sent Him.

21-27   Jesus became broken in spirit as He contemplated Judas' deception. Despite not being one of His own, He loved him. Then He announced another critical truth.

> I tell you the truth, one of you is going to betray me.

Those who betray their faith for a favour will always be present, even in Jesus' presence. The disciples were perplexed, who among them would do such a thing? They asked John (the disciple Jesus loved) to find out.

Reclining at table was not seated as we understand it. The table was a few inches off the floor and the diners would lay on their left side propped on an elbow, legs and body laying at an angle from the table. John was on Jesus' right. So as John rotated back to talk to Jesus, His head would be on Jesus' breast. Leaning back this way, John was able to ask the question, "Lord, who is it?"

It seems that only John heard the answer, as the disciples did not know what Judas was about to do. But Judas surely knew. Judas took the bread and "Satan entered into him." This work of the devil was not left to a lesser demon; Satan anticipated this was to be his finest hour, and he would personally direct operations.

While the disciples wondered why Judas went out, John commented, "And it was night." As Jesus commented earlier, "Night is coming when no man can work," 9:4. The night was symbolic of the darkness that had enveloped Judas.

Jesus Predicts Peter's Denial

31-33   Judas left, and Jesus became more intimate with the eleven. His first words indicated the imminent approach of His glory as the Son of Man. The One to whom was given all authority, worship and an everlasting kingdom in Daniel's vision, Daniel 7:13-14, was about to lay the groundwork to accomplish that vision.

Initially, that glory was the cross, the place of the defeat of Satan, the accomplishment of His mission. A few days later Jesus Christ would rise from the dead in His glorified body as John reveals later in his gospel.

The sense of indivisibility comes through clearly. The Father would glorify Him, and in doing so, would glorify Himself. But Jesus, by His death and resurrection would also glorify the Father. Whatever the Son or the Father do directly affects the other, for they are one.

Jesus' journey was one that His disciples could not follow—at least immediately. He would be with them only two days longer, and He would be crucified. But note His address to them as "my children." His concern for them is that of a parent for his child.

34–38 The command to love one another seems simple and obvious enough to us. In fact, the command was already given in the Old Testament, Deuteronomy 6:5 and Leviticus 19:18. Jesus expanded on it: "As I have loved you, so you must love one another." His love was to die for them. That sacrificial love between believers would draw men and women to Christ.

Peter sidestepped the love angle, wanting to know more about where Jesus was going. Jesus' answer was revealing. Peter could not follow Jesus "now," but will follow "later." As Jesus revealed later, Peter would eventually die for his faith in Christ, 21:19, but only after a period of maturing as His apostle (messenger).

Peter would eventually lay down his life for Christ, but in the meantime, the reverse would be true as Jesus announced this critical truth specifically for Peter:

I tell you the truth, before the rooster crows, you will disown me three times!

Whatever Peter's protestations of faithfulness, it would not be infallible.

14

Jesus Shows the Way to the Father and Begins Teaching on the Holy Spirit.

**"I am the way and the truth and the life.
No one comes to the Father except through me."**

John 14:6

This chapter continues the upper room discourse, but moves from the distressing predictions of denial and Jesus' going away to the intimate knowledge of God and the coming Holy Spirit. The future comfort and direction of the Holy Spirit would be a direct result of faith in Jesus Christ and His oneness with the Father.

Jesus Shows the Way to the Father

1–4 Jesus' words in the last chapter would have distressed the disciples, so Jesus invited them to trust Him, as they trusted God. Eventually they would have a permanent place with Him. The Father's "house" is, of course, more than a house, but a mansion, the New Jerusalem that would come to earth, Revelation 21:10.

In that place, many dwelling places would be ready for them following Jesus' ascension and His second coming. Jesus will return to collect His own and take them to be with Him "that you also may be where I am." Then Jesus finished with a challenge: "You know the way to the place where I am going."

5–8   Thomas, clearly confused, asked how they could know the way if they did not know the destination. Then Jesus made His well-known declaration, with emphatic force, "*I am the way and the truth and the life.*" This all-encompassing title confirmed that Jesus was the route to heaven, simply by belief in Him. He had the only and all truth. Life—here and beyond—was only to be found in Him. "No one comes to the Father except through me."

This statement has always been criticized as exclusive, on the belief that it denies other ways to God. But as Jesus is the Truth, there is no other way. But it is inclusive, for all are welcome, none need be excluded except by their own unbelief in Jesus, the Truth. Then Jesus finishes again with another challenge, referring to the Father, "From now on, you do know Him and have seen Him."

9–13   Phillip rose to the bait, asking for a revelation of the Father. The slowness of the disciples to understand Jesus irked Him. Jesus gave the simple answer, "Anyone who has seen me has seen the Father." In the next few verses, Jesus deepens the claim that He and the Father are one, each resides in the other. Thus Jesus speaks God's words and does His work. At least, Jesus advises, "believe on the evidence of the miracles themselves."

Referring back to the miracles He has done, Jesus declared that anyone with faith in Him will continue His work. On this basis, Jesus stated a further critical truth:

I tell you the truth, anyone who has faith in me will do what I have been doing. He will do even greater things than these, because I am going to the Father.

Already, after Pentecost, thousands began to believe in Jesus, be baptized and enter His kingdom. Since then, the faith and prayers of His people have changed the direction of the world several times, and individuals' lives the world over have been changed.

But these "greater things" are not wrought simply by appending the name of Jesus to a prayer. They occur from prayers and commitment to fulfill the purpose of God in this world. Recall that part of the Lord's Prayer that sets out God's purpose for this planet, "Your Kingdom come, your will be done on earth as it is in heaven." As we pray for those things and work toward building His Kingdom, He will provide what we need.

Jesus Begins His Teaching on the Holy Spirit

15–18　　　Here Jesus begins a series of teachings on the Holy Spirit. We will find more in succeeding chapters. But these verses also have ten references to love. We will discuss this relationship to love and obedience as we look at these and some later verses.

Jesus has spoken often of His love for His own, but now He spoke of those who love Him. Verse 15 links love with obedience. Belief has its consequences, and the way we live betrays what we really believe. These two ideals are opposite sides of the same coin. When our youngest daughter was in trouble she would say, "Daddy, I love you," hoping to soften my heart. My response was, "If you love me, do as I say."

We cannot love God without showing it by our obedience. In verse 21, Jesus and the Father respond in love to the one who loves and obeys the Son. Further in verse 23, not only did Jesus repeat the response of love for the one who loves and obeys, but that both Jesus and the Father will "make our home with him."

In verse 24, the reverse is also true. Those who do not love will not obey—"by their fruit you will recognise them," Matthew 7:20. Jesus is the supreme example; He loves the Father and does what He asks, verse 31.

The New Testament clearly states that our obedient works do not save us. Only by faith in the atoning work of Jesus

Christ on Calvary are we reconciled to God. Works cannot *procure* salvation, but they are a subsequent *evidence* of the faith that saves us.

16-18   This is the first promise of the Holy Spirit coming to believers. We have already noted the Holy Spirit came upon Jesus at His baptism, and that Jesus would eventually baptise His followers in the Holy Spirit, 1:33. On that occasion, all three members of the Trinity were present: Jesus who was being baptised, the Spirit who rested upon Him, and the voice of the Father extolling the Son.

All three are also mentioned together in this passage, and later in verse 26. The response of the Spirit in coming into the world shows all three in agreement that the Spirit is a gift of both Father and Son. The coming of "another" is not a simple replacement, but an exact representation of the Son as the Son exactly represents the Father.

In these verses, John reports the Spirit would come as a "Counsellor," literally translated as, "One who comes alongside." He would be with them "forever," and would be the "Spirit of truth." No truth is found outside of Jesus Christ. Jesus came to "testify to the truth," 18:37, and the Holy Spirit would further that purpose, as John records later, convicting of sin and drawing people to Christ.

The world will not accept Him, for it prefers its own path and follows Satan's lies, recall 8:43-45. But in the same way that Jesus' sheep know His voice, 10:14, so they will know the Spirit. At that point He will be "with you," but later—probably referring to the Day of Pentecost—He would be "in you," indwelling all believers.

The promise of the Holy Spirit meant Jesus would "not leave you as orphans." The Spirit would take the Son's place until His final return for His own, 14:3.

19-21   Jesus predicted He would reappear to His disciples following His resurrection. Those who rejected Him would not see Him again; disbelieving in His resurrection would obscure their ability to recognize Him.

But His appearance to the disciples after His resurrection would confirm Jesus was the source of life—death had no hold on Him—and their life was secure in Him. Not only that, but like the enfolding of the Father and Son we mentioned in the previous passage, 14:10, Jesus now includes His disciples in that enfolded relationship.

Love is the key to that relationship. The Father and Son were in complete agreement on purpose and strategy. The Father and Son will love those, who in agreement with the disciples, love and obey Christ. Furthermore, Christ will "show myself to him"; an inner conviction by the Holy Spirit of the full identity of Christ.

22-24 To the disciples' view—that Jesus was to be their political earthly deliverer—it didn't make sense that Jesus would not show Himself to the world. Jesus' answer was in keeping with His plan to redeem His own—those who love Him and obey His teaching. Jesus' Kingdom "is not of this world. If it were, my servants would fight . . ." 18:36.

But those who do love Jesus Christ will become the residence of both the Son and the Father, by the indwelling Spirit. Those who do not love the Son will be recognised by speech and action opposed to Christ's teaching. Jesus' teaching was not His own, but came from the Father.

25-27 The lack of the disciples' spiritual awareness meant Jesus had more to teach them, note 16:12. The Holy Spirit would continue Jesus' instruction. But notice the importance placed on being reminded by the Holy Spirit. Much of the disciples learning was not new revelation but later recalling Jesus' words with fresh understanding.

Christians mature in the faith by knowing God's word, which the Spirit is able to use for His purposes. Ignorance of the Scriptures hinders the Spirit's work. This knowledge of

Jesus' words would inspire and comfort during the difficult years of ministry ahead for the disciples.

Thus Jesus was able to offer His disciples peace. Peace for the world is a longing or wish. But salvation in Jesus Christ is an inner settled rest of spirit, a sense of well-being centred in Him. This alleviates fear and distress in all circumstances of life. Storms may erupt on the surface, but there is still that sense of calm below. Recall 2 Timothy 1:7: "God did not give us a spirit of timidity, but a spirit of power, of love, and of self-discipline."

28-31 Jesus predicted His going away and return. For the immediate future, it would mean His death and resurrection. They would see Him again for a short period when He arose. But He also spoke of going to the Father which meant a permanent separation. If the disciples loved Him, they would be glad for Him. Not only would Jesus' suffering be over, but He would return to the Father who loved Him.

But Jesus' return would also be good for the disciples. Jesus was limited by His humanity, and His ministry depended on the greater power given from the Father. At His ascension, Jesus would return to His former glory and His ministry extended accordingly.

Jesus' predictions about Himself also encouraged the disciples' faith as they saw those predictions fulfilled, necessary because He would not be with them much longer. Jesus warned that Satan, although defeated at the cross, would still be around to influence those who reject Christ, but he had no hold on the sinless Son of God.

Whatever Satan's strategy, Jesus remained firm that He fulfilled His Father's directions and the world will eventually learn that Jesus and the Father are one in love and there is no truth apart from them.

15

Jesus the True Vine and Expecting Persecution

You did not choose me, but I chose you and appointed you to go and bear fruit—fruit that will last. Then the Father will give you whatever you ask in my name.

John 15:16

This chapter deals with Jesus as the vine, which is one of the best-known passages in John's gospel. Jesus also extended this passage to review again the need for love, as it is needful to remain in Him. Jesus also warned His disciples that as He was persecuted His followers must expect the same.

Staying in the Vine

1–4   Jesus opened this passage by asserting, "I *am* the true vine. Once again, His emphasis is on truth; there is no other source of life. Furthermore, the Father is the gardener, and a good gardener cares for the vine and the fruit it will bear.

But already in verse 2, Jesus warned of judgment. The purpose of the vine is to produce grapes, and any branch which does not do so, will be cut from the tree. Those branches are most probably counterfeit Christians, like Judas Iscariot. The fruit God desires is that which extends His

107

Kingdom, and is only possible when attached to the vine. Fruit is not something the vine strives for, but emerges naturally when drawing its life from the vine.

However, fruitful branches are pruned to produce more fruit. Pruning is not always comfortable, and may feel like judgment at times! The verb "prune" can be also be translated "clean," and Jesus taught here it is belief in His word that cleanses. Word here is translated from logos and refers to the whole word–in fact, Jesus is the Word, 1:1. Remaining in Him means committed to continuing belief in Him and His word.

Unless His disciples remained in Him, they would not bear fruit. The question arises, what fruit? We are not told here, but suggestions from Scripture are souls for the Kingdom, the fruit of the Spirit, Galatians 5:22-23, or influence for Christ, whether we are conscious of it or not.

5–8   Jesus again used the emphatic version of "I am," as He repeats, "I *am* the vine." He is not only the true vine, but also the permanent one. All other claims for life are temporary and will pass away with the old earth. Recall Jesus' words concerning His return, Matthew 24:35, "Heaven and earth will pass away, but my words will never pass away." Remaining in Him, a man or woman will bear much fruit.

At this point Jesus returned to judgment. The lifeless branches were cut off and burned, a horrific reference to the consuming fire of hell, about which Jesus talked elsewhere; for instance, Matthew 5:22, and John's description in Revelation 20:14.

Before Jesus changed the subject, He promised to give whatever they ask if they remained in His words. These words are rhemata, the individual sayings of Jesus the Spirit would later bring to mind, 14:26. Clearly, answers will not include any selfish or sinful desire, but those prayers that conform to His word entrenched in His disciples. The answer to those prayers will produce more fruit and glorify the Father.

Love Each Other

9–12   Jesus pointed out that He had loved the disciples as the Father loved Him. The evidence of His love was His obedience to the Father. He wanted the disciples to remain in His love in the same way, by obeying His teaching. He set the pattern for them.

The outcome of loving in this way is joy. We mentioned earlier, happiness is the outcome of selfless service. But we must separate joy from happiness. Happiness relates to happenings: a new car, the birth of a child, falling in love and so on. Joy is a permanent state of mind irrespective of circumstances, akin to peace, 14:27. The security and sure hope in Christ transcends earthly matters. The world knows nothing like it. So Paul encouraged us, "Rejoice in the Lord always. I will say it again: rejoice," Philippians 4:4. And this joy is wrapped up in this: "Love each other as I have loved you."

13–17   Jesus laid down His life for us and He taught this was the greatest love. This self-giving is the basis of all relationships. Furthermore, friendship has no secrets. Servants' knowledge of their master's business is on a need to know basis. But Jesus divulged to His disciples all the Father passed to Him, although this would be an unfolding revelation, 16:12-13.

The disciples were not a random collection of followers, but chosen by Christ for specific work. What seemed like a ragtag group became the fiercest devotees to His cause. Their fruit, continued through the centuries, is incalculable. It was as they sought His Kingdom first, Matthew 6:33, and by their love for each other, their prayers were answered.

Jesus Warns of Persecution

18–21   We have seen evidence of the hatred of the Jews toward Jesus, and much more was yet to come. The idea of two worlds: an earth only based reality, and the Kingdom of heaven comes through clearly in this section. Once we are translated into Christ's Kingdom, the world's focus no longer draws us; we do not belong there.

The reason the world hates the followers of Jesus Christ is the disciples' preoccupation with the Kingdom of God. As Jesus said, they hated and persecuted Him first, and so they will hate and persecute His disciples also, because "no servant is greater than his master."

But the opposite is also true: those who accept Christ's teaching will also accept the disciples' teaching. As Jesus often noted previously, those who persecute Jesus and His followers do so because they do not know God.

22–27 Jesus' appearance on earth, His works and words from the Father, established the guilt of those who rejected Him, for those who rejected Him also rejected the Father. The knowledge of Jesus, His miracles, and His word, was a privilege that carried greater responsibility. The response of hatred, Jesus pointed out, was for the Father as well as Him. Jesus, by way of emphasis, repeats this claim.

Then Jesus notes that they have no reason to hate Him. Why should they? He came to save them. But just as David had his enemies without cause, Psalms 35:19 and 69:4, so it was fulfilled toward Jesus.

Jesus reverts to the coming of the Holy Spirit, the Spirit of truth, begun previously in chapter 14. Despite the persecution they would face, the disciples were to testify about Jesus because they knew Him best, "You have been with me since the beginning." In addition, they would have the help of the Holy Spirit who would also testify to the truth of Jesus Christ through them. They would not be alone.

16

The Work of the Holy Spirit

**I will see you again and you will rejoice,
and no one will take away your joy.**

John 16:22

In this chapter, Jesus desires to comfort His disciples at the news He will be leaving them. He does this by recalling the promise of the Holy Spirit, by discussing the "little while" He will be absent yet their joy at seeing Him again, and finally by confirming their inclusion with Him in the Father.

1–4   Persecution, and lucid arguments against the faith accepted by the majority, are likely to persuade the wavering. Being prepared for persecution would help stabilise their faith. In fact, persecution would confirm it.

As history has clearly established, the religious establishment would often be the persecutors, believing they were performing God's will. Despite their religious claims, the Father is not the God they serve, for they "have not known the Father or me."

Now Jesus would be going away, He tells His disciples He needs to warn them of persecution so they would remember His words "when the time comes." Persecution is the usual state of those who follow Jesus.

5–7   The disciples avoided questioning Jesus about where He would be going; they did not want to talk about it. As Jesus pointed out, "You are filled with grief." So now Jesus set out another critical truth:

> *I tell you the truth: It is for your good that I am going away. Unless I go away, the Counsellor will not come to you; but if I go, I will send Him to you.*

Jesus informed the disciples He needed to leave before the Holy Spirit could come and be with them. The plan of salvation must be complete before Jesus left. When the Holy Spirit came, He would have a wider ministry than Jesus for the remainder of earth's history, not limited as Jesus was by His temporary humanity.

8–11   The Holy Spirit's work in the world is threefold, demonstrated by the three references to the Holy Spirit in Genesis. He creates, Genesis 1:2, He convicts of sin, Genesis 6:3, and He indwells His people, Genesis 41:38.

This threefold work of the Spirit is confirmed in the New Testament. The Holy Spirit created Jesus in the womb of Mary and creates new life in the believer. He also convicts as we read in this chapter, and He indwells the believer as recorded on the day of Pentecost, Acts 2:4.

In this passage, Jesus concentrates on the convicting work of the Holy Spirit by exposing the guilt of the world. He will convict of sin, because men refuse to believe in Jesus Christ. The greatest sin is to reject Jesus Christ, for it is to reject God.

All other sin flows from it. The Spirit will bring awareness of the righteousness of Jesus Christ, because the Father has accepted Him and His work in obtaining salvation for the world. Finally, the judgement of Satan is evidence and a preview of judgement to come.

12–15   Now Jesus began to teach how the Spirit's work in convicting the world would also work in convincing the disciples of the truth. After all, the Spirit is the Spirit of truth.

The disciples needed to mature to be able to accept deeper truth. In addition, they needed their minds opened to further truth the Spirit would unfold.

Note the sequence of the Spirit's message. He would bring glory to Christ, which is the Spirit's purpose, by sharing what He hears from Jesus. But what the Spirit hears from Jesus is what Jesus has shared from the Father. So the Spirit will reveal and convince the truth concerning the Father and the Son.

Paul expands on this in 1 Corinthians 2:5-14. "No mind has conceived what God has prepared for those who love Him, but God has revealed it to us by His Spirit." Paul goes on to explain that the "natural man without the Spirit does not accept the things that come from the Spirit of God, for they are foolishness to him, and he cannot understand them for they are spiritually discerned." However, Paul reminds us, "we have the mind of Christ."

The work of the Spirit is to bring understanding of spiritual things to the believer. The Holy Spirit has already inspired the writers of Scripture. Now He illumines the mind of the reader, for unregenerate minds cannot conceive of spiritual things.

16-22   Now Jesus turned to further comforting the disciples by speaking of the "little while," commonly understood as the period between the crucifixion and Jesus' resurrection. But Jesus had two things in mind, not only His short residence in the grave, but also that He would be returning to the Father. These sayings of Jesus left the disciples confused.

Jesus went on to explain that this time of pain for Him, and mourning for the disciples, would give place to a new joy that would remain. Jesus emphasized tis critical truth:

> I tell you the truth, you will weep and mourn while the
> world rejoices. You will grieve, but your grief will turn
> to joy.

Jesus explained to the disciples what is true for all who trust Him: the period of pain they experience will one day be

113

turned to joy—if not in this life, certainly in the next. "You will rejoice, and no one will take away your joy." Jesus used the example of childbirth, the pain of which is forgotten when the child is born, recall Psalm 30:5. Jesus would be gone for a "little while" but afterwards they would see Him again, either after His resurrection, or when they meet Him again in glory.

23–24   After that time, and concurrent with the disciple's joy at Jesus' resurrection, they would experience the value of praying "in Jesus name." This, of course, was not simply a tagline attached to their prayers, but confirmed the prayers were made within Jesus' purpose for the world. Then He stated a further critical truth:

> *I tell you the truth, my Father will give you whatever*
> *you ask in my name. Until now you have not asked for*
> *anything in my name. Ask and you will receive, and*
> *your joy will be complete.*

Recall the prayer Jesus gave to His disciples: "Your Kingdom come, your will be done on earth as it is in heaven," Matthew 6:10. Note Jesus twice used the phrase "in my name." Those prayers would be answered and bring joy to the disciples.

25–30   In these verses, Jesus began to speak about His return to the Father. Then, the disciples will ask the Father—again in the name of Jesus—and the Father will answer their prayers because He loves them as they have loved His Son.

The disciples began to understand Jesus ministry in plain words, and saw the extent of Jesus ministry. "Now we can see that you know all things," and this revelation confirmed their belief that Jesus came from God.

31–33   Jesus' delight in their new understanding drew Him to return to the subject of His crucifixion. For that short time they would be scattered, "each to his own home." Although Jesus would be left alone, the Father would continue to be with Him.

This would also be true for the disciples in their ministry. They would have trouble, but the continued presence of the Father and the Holy Spirit indwelling them would bring them peace. Note the opposing places: "in the world," and "in Him." Whatever they faced in the future, their trust in Jesus would never be betrayed for He said "I have overcome the world."

17

Jesus Prays to the Father

Now this is eternal life: that they may know you, the only true God, and Jesus Christ, whom you have sent.

John 17:3

It is fitting that Jesus' discourse to the disciples should end in prayer. It is one thing to teach, but prayer is essential to ensure what they learned would be effective and lasting.

This chapter contains Jesus' longest recorded prayer, and divides into three distinct parts: Jesus prays for Himself–notably the shortest section, then He prays for His disciples, and prays for all believers.

Jesus Prays for Himself

1-5   Jesus asks God to glorify Him now "the time has come." Recall frequent references to Jesus' time had not yet come, earlier in the Gospel: 2:4, 7:6, 8, 30, 8:20. These verses explain Christ's glory as "authority over all people," recall Daniel 7:14.

But His glory is also to "give eternal life to all those you have given Him." Jesus has the authority to determine the future of all people, but His greatest joy is to give eternal life to those who believe.

To bring glory also means to honour, "I have brought you glory by completing the work you gave me to do." Jesus' desire was that men and women should know the Father, for eternal life is "that they may know you, the only true God, and Jesus Christ, whom you have sent."

But Jesus also asked the Father to glorify Him. The Father would honour Jesus for His sacrificial atonement at the cross, and vindicate Him by His resurrection and ascension back to the Father. The glory of the Father and Son are bound together as each honours and glorifies the other.

As these verses close, Jesus gives the clearest indication of His deity yet, "glorify me in your presence with the glory I had with you *before the world began*," (my emphasis). Jesus looked forward to His reunification with the Father at His coming ascension.

Jesus Prays for His Disciples

6–8   In these verses, Jesus emphasizes that all He has accomplished comes from the Father. Note the following phrases in which Jesus lists the progress His disciples made during His time with them.

I have revealed you to those whom you gave me

They were yours (before the world began, (Ephesians 1:4)

They obeyed your word

They know that everything I have comes from you

I gave them the words you gave me and they accepted them

They knew with certainty I came from you

They believed that you sent me

Jesus rejoiced with the Father at these authentic marks of Christianity these men had achieved. They were also essential requirements for the disciples' future ministry.

9–12   Jesus confirmed His unity with the Father while in human flesh, "all I have is yours and all you have is mine." Jesus and the Father are co-equal in the Trinity, but Jesus totally depended on the Father while He put His personal glory aside.

On this occasion, Jesus prayed for His disciples, not for the world. Jesus was concerned for protection of His disciples from the world after He had gone. Although He faced the cross and resurrection, He was aware and sure of His return to the Father.

His protection of the disciples (except for Judas Iscariot) was not necessarily physical, but primarily spiritual—they would remain faithful and secure in Christ, verse 15. That protection would be by "the power of your name." That name, given to Jesus, enabled Him to keep them safe from the evil one.

13–16   Jesus prayed the disciples would continue to experience the same joy when He is gone they gained from Him in His earthly presence; necessary because now they have received and believed Jesus word, the world will hate them.

Now they were not of the world, its attitudes to this life and worldly direction, their focus is on spiritual things in the world to come. However, His prayer for them was not that they be taken from the world, because they would serve the world by continuing the ministry of Jesus after He left.

17–19   Now Jesus prayed for the disciples' sanctification. To be sanctified, made holy, simply means being set apart, to be separate. Salvation is one thing—to be reconciled to God through the sacrifice of Jesus Christ. But sanctification is an ongoing process. "Sanctify them by the truth; your word is truth."

Awareness and acceptance of, and witness to Jesus Christ, Himself the truth, is the basis for an effective and productive life committed to building God's Kingdom.

Jesus Prays for All Believers

20–23   The disciples' continued witness to the truth was essential so others would also believe. Jesus now prayed for those later believers all down the centuries to our age and beyond. He asked the Father that future believers in Him would also be in the Son and Father as they, the Father and Son are in one another. The unity of the Father and Son is their nature, and this unity of them with all believers would be the evidence to the world of Jesus' identity.

Furthermore, the disciples would share in Christ's glory, where they will be one with the Father and Son. It would also demonstrate the love Jesus had for them, and the world He came to save.

24–26   Jesus reiterated His desire that believers would share in His glory, "to be where I am." The Father loved Jesus and gave Him His glory "before the creation of the world." Although the world does not know the Father, Jesus does, and all believers know Jesus comes from the Father.

Despite praying for future disciples, Jesus used the past tense to demonstrate He has already made the Father known to them, and "will continue to make you known in order that the love you have for me may be in them and that I myself may be in them." A promise to all of us.

18

Jesus is Arrested and Tried and Peter Denies Jesus

For this reason I was born, and for this I came into the world, to testify to the truth. Everyone on the side of truth listens to me."

John 18:37

The previous chapters of John we have studied were mostly teaching by Jesus. The chapters that follow are descriptions of the arrest, crucifixion, and resurrection of Jesus. The other gospels provide more information on these events, but we will stick with John's account unless relevant information from the other gospels is helpful. In the earlier part of the chapter, we read of Jesus' arrest and questioning by the high priest. For ease of reference, we will put Peter's three denials together and not separated as in the Bible passage.

Jesus' Arrest

1–3 Jesus was arrested immediately following His prayer for His disciples and those who followed them. He went with His disciples to the olive grove where He knew Judas would find Him. Even knowing that His crucifixion was imminent, He actively moved towards it, not away from it.

Judas took no chances. He was fully aware of Jesus' miraculous powers, and he brought with him a detachment of Roman soldiers, plus officials from the Jews. The officials were there to ensure Jesus' arrest, and Roman soldiers were necessary because only the Romans could administer capital punishment that the Jews sought.

4–9   Jesus offered no resistance, not because He was guilty or innocent, but because He knew the next few hours were the Father's will. He confronted the soldiers and officials to ensure He was the one they sought and their answer confirmed it.

Jesus replied, "I *am* He." The words "I am" were emphatic as we have noted in previous chapters, with their connection to Exodus 3:14. The result was dramatic. The soldiers, those with them, and Judas, drew back and fell to the ground under the power of those words. John repeats the words, "I *am* He" three times, emphasizing their importance.

Jesus repeated His question, and receiving the same answer, again stated, "I *am* He." This time Jesus withheld the power of those words and He was taken into custody. But His concern for the disciples was such that He requested that they be let go. John adds, "that the words He had spoken would be fulfilled: 'I have not lost one of those you gave me,'" see 6:39, 17:12. Jesus protected His disciples to the end. Not only did He pray for them, but also took practical action when required.

10–11   Peter, impetuous as ever, decided to intervene and he sliced off the ear of the high priest's servant. Peter, probably motivated by his previous claim he would lay down his life for Jesus, and Jesus' response of Peter's denials, decided this was his chance to make good his claim.

Jesus rebuked Peter for two reasons. First, Jesus had to go through this sacrifice set out before Him; "Shall I not drink the cup the Father has given me?" Second, as Jesus pointed out later in verse 36, His Kingdom is beyond this world; it does not require earthly violence to protect it.

Matthew 22:51 tells us that Jesus healed the man's ear. Even that miracle before the eyes of the arresting party had no effect on them.

Jesus' Trials before the High Priest

12-14   Jesus was arrested, bound, and taken to the high priest's house. The high priest's position was for his lifetime, but the Romans had previously deposed Annas as high priest. Caiaphas, Annas' son-in-law, had taken his place and was high priest that year as John records.

Jesus' appearance before Annas and Caiaphas was a preliminary examination before they sent Jesus to Pilate, the Roman governor, for judgment. Only the Roman governor could authorize an execution. John recalls that Caiaphas was the one who had predicted that Jesus should die for the sake of the nation. Thus, it was most likely that Caiaphas was not interested in a fair trial, but was seeking Jesus' execution.

To maintain events together, we will temporarily pass over Peter's first denial and continue with the trial by Annas.

19-24   John records the investigation by Annas. Although deposed by the Romans, Annas was still in high regard by the Jews as the real high priest. This was probably the first time for Annas to interview Jesus, although he had certainly heard much about Him.

Annas questioned Jesus about His disciples and teaching, probably hoping for Jesus to make some traitorous statement. In answer, Jesus made a factual statement that He had always spoken and taught publicly. Thus, there were witnesses the high priest could call to judge Jesus.

An official struck Jesus for insolence. However, Jesus made the point that the official should provide witness to what, if anything, Jesus had done wrong. Jesus' call for witness before the high priest and the official who struck Him was an

123

important request for proper legal representation, for a person could only be convicted through genuine witnesses.

Note Jesus' calm response to the official's attack. He didn't respond in anger or berate the official, but simply responded with a statement of fact. This concluded the examination before Annas, and He was passed to Caiaphas for further examination. John does not record the examination before Caiaphas, but it is recorded in the other gospels.

Peter's Denials

15–18   We return now to the passages that record Peter's denials. Peter and another disciple went into the courtyard of the high priest. That other disciple was almost certainly John, who does not refer to himself by name in his gospel, but by the expression: the disciple that Jesus loved. See references in 13:23, and 20:2.

John was known to some in the high priest's retinue, and went inside the courtyard to get approval for Peter to come in. But the servant girl guarding the gate challenged Peter to ensure he was not one of Jesus' disciples. Peter was caught off guard and without thinking, simply said, "I am not," perhaps simply to ensure admittance to the courtyard.

It is doubtful Peter was in any real danger; even after cutting off the servant's ear earlier, no one had been interested in him; with the ear healed, there was little evidence of Peter's attack. Peter joined John and the other officials gathered around the fire to keep warm. It is worth mentioning that John didn't seem fearful, perhaps recognizing the Jews were interested in Jesus, not His followers, and the authorities had agreed to Jesus' request to let them go.

25–27   Around the fire, Peter was questioned again about his relationship to Jesus. However, having denied once, the second time was easy to continue the same convenient denial he gave at the gate.

The third challenge seemed more dangerous, for the questioner knew the man Peter had injured. If Peter was fearful, this only added to his fear and for the third time he denied knowing Jesus Christ. Then the cock crowed and Peter remembered Jesus' earlier prediction of his denials, 13:38.

Luke gives an emotional insight: "The Lord turned and looked straight at Peter. Then Peter remembered the word the Lord had spoken to him: 'Before the rooster crows today, you will disown me three times.' And he went outside and wept bitterly," Luke 22:61–62.

The Trial Before Pilate

28–32   The Jews brought Jesus to Pilate early on Friday morning, the first day of Passover, but refused to enter his palace as this would render them unclean for the rest of the week's Passover festivities. Recall that for the Jews, each day begins at 6.00 p.m. in the evening. Thus, Jesus had celebrated Passover with His disciples the evening before, although many would celebrate later that evening. The irony of the situation was their total defilement in seeking the death of Jesus their Messiah.

They came to the Roman Governor, as he was the only one who could authorise a death sentence. Pilate naturally asked what charge they were bringing against Jesus. The Jews considered their trials were sufficient to warrant the death penalty. However, Pilate was opening a new trial, not just confirming their trials.

However, the Jews had no specific charge that would stand up in Roman law—no Roman charge, no Roman trial. Their only answer was ambiguous: "If He were not a criminal we would not have handed Him over to you."

Pilate's simple response was for them to judge him by their own law. The Jews replied they had no authority to execute anyone. John notes their answer confirmed how Jesus had predicted He would die, 12:32–33. "Lifted up" meant crucifixion, the Roman means of execution. The Jewish method of execution was stoning.

33–37   Pilate went inside to question Jesus himself. By asking if Jesus was the "King of the Jews," Pilate thought he might pin sedition on Jesus as an enemy of Caesar. Jesus asked if that was Pilate's own idea. If it was Pilate's idea, then Pilate was asking if He was a rebel. If the Jews told him, then it meant, was He a king of the Jews only, like Herod? If so, it was an internal Jewish question.

Pilate did not want to be embroiled in Jewish controversy, but Pilate still needed to find out what Jesus had done that might contravene Roman law. Jesus was not willing to incriminate Himself, so He set His Kingdom beyond this world. He didn't need soldiers to fight for it, it "is from another place."

Jesus agreed with Pilate, "You are right in saying I am a king." But Jesus' authority lay not in power but in truth. "For this reason I was born, and for this I came into the world, to testify to the truth." Note the sequence: "born," became a man; "came into the world," established His pre-existence; His mission, the truth.

As creator, truth originates with God, and Jesus claimed, "I *am* . . . the truth." 14:6. Then naturally, it follows that, "Everyone on the side of truth listens to me." The truth about all creation and existence upon which we must build our lives, is also the basis of the cosmic battle that engages us all: for or against accountability to our Creator.

38–40   Pilate's response, "What is truth?" appeared one of disdain; then, and now, truth seemed sufficiently elusive to be unattainable. However, Pilate concluded Jesus was innocent–teaching truth was not a criminal offence.

Pilate hoped he had a way out. It was a custom for the Romans to release a prisoner, and releasing Jesus would shelve the matter. However, the Jews wanted Barabbas, a known rebel and murderer, over Jesus, the author of life.

19

The Crucifixion of Jesus Christ

The man who saw it has given testimony, and his testimony is true. He knows that he tells the truth, and he testifies so that you also may believe.

John 19:35

John wanted to make it clear he was an eyewitness of Jesus' crucifixion and that Jesus was dead. Without evidence of Jesus' death, the resurrection could always be challenged.

The Judgment

1–7   Pilate had Jesus flogged. Although innocent of any crime, He was still the centre of a disturbance. Perhaps Pilate hoped this would satisfy the Jews. For a second time, Pilate announced Jesus' innocence, "I find no basis for a charge against Him," see 18:38.

After a cruel flogging, abuse, and humiliation, and wearing a mockery of kingship–a crown of thorns and purple robe, Pilate brought Jesus out before the Jews again. "Here is the man," he said, Jesus hardly the spectacle of a king or a dangerous rebel. But without reason, the chief priests and officials demanded He be crucified.

For a third time, Pilate confirmed his finding of Jesus' innocence, and insisted a second time on the Jews to deal with Him according to their own laws. This could not include the death penalty, but the Jews insisted that Jesus deserved to die, "Because He claimed to be the Son of God," blasphemy according to their unbelief.

8–11   This increased Pilate's fear. The Roman belief in families of gods made Jesus a possible god, which prompted the question, "Where do you come from?" Jesus had already given that information, 18:35, and remained silent. Pilate, irritated at Jesus' silence, warned he had power "either to free you or to crucify you." This claim admitted Pilate's responsibility for Jesus' death.

At this point, Pilate suppressed the truth he had heard, compare Romans 1:18. Furthermore, Pilate's authority came from above, Proverbs 8:15, Romans 13:1, and God would judge his performance in accord or not with God's purpose for the earth, Matthew 6:10.

God who gave Pilate his ruling authority also limited his power. Jesus declared His own ultimate authority, "You would have no power over me if it were not given to you from above."

Jesus' death was a willing death within God's overall plan. But that did not absolve those who engineered His death, primarily Caiaphas and the leading Jews who had the Scriptures to enlighten them. They were guilty of the greater sin. But Pilate was also guilty to a lesser degree.

12–16   Pilate endeavoured to free Jesus. The Jews countered with the claim, "Anyone who claims to be a king opposes Caesar." Finally, Pilate came to his judgment as he took his judge's seat.

Pilate presented Jesus for the final time, "Here is your king." But the Jews continued to demand Jesus' crucifixion; they denied He was their king. Not to do so risked rebellion against Caesar. The Jews used Pilate's fear of Caesar to persuade him to their view. He faced the same decision we all face: who is the king of our lives?

Therefore, against his own conclusion of Jesus' innocence, 18:38, 19:4 and 6, Pilate handed Jesus over for crucifixion without just cause. Telling the truth was not a crime.

The Crucifixion of Jesus

17–18　Crucifixion was a Roman execution, so Roman soldiers took Jesus to Golgotha, also known as Calvary. John notes that Jesus carried His own cross, suggesting by his language it was a deliberate action of control on Jesus' part, despite coercion to carry His own cross until His strength gave out.

Matthew chapter 27 recounts the crucifixion and death of Jesus. It records Simon ordered to carry the cross as Jesus' loss of blood from His flogging made Him too weak to carry it. Matthew also records that Jesus, when crucified, refused to drink a mixture of wine and myrrh, used to reduce the pain. He would not turn away from the suffering needed to redeem us.

Jesus was crucified between two thieves, fulfilling the prophecy that He was "numbered with the transgressors," Isaiah 53:12. His crucifixion took place at on Friday 9.00 a.m. the third hour in the other gospels, but the sixth hour according to John's use of Roman time.

Matthew also reports Jesus endured mocking from the crowd around Him, but He refused to respond. In addition, the chief priests taunted Him: "He saved others," they said, "but He can't save Himself! He's the King of Israel! Let Him come down now from the cross, and we will believe in Him. He trusts in God. Let God rescue Him now if He wants Him, for He said, 'I am the Son of God,'" Matthew 27:42–44.

Luke, in chapter 23, adds He prayed for those who crucified Him, and responded to the need of one of the criminals crucified with Him.

19–24　The sign above the cross stated His crime. In Jesus' case, Pilate used the Jews' own charge as he had cleared Jesus of any Roman crime. The crucifixion was in a public place where it warned others not to rock the Roman boat. Pilate also used the sign to insult and infuriate the Jews, and he refused to change the wording.

Those crucified were humiliated by being stripped naked, and the soldiers claimed the clothes, sharing Jesus' clothes among them. The soldiers cast lots for His seamless undergarment, fulfilling the Scripture, "They divide my garments among them and cast lots for my clothing," Psalm 22:18.

Isaiah in his prophecy described Jesus' appearance: "There were many who were appalled at Him—His appearance was so disfigured beyond that of any man and His form marred beyond human likeness," Isaiah 52:14, and "He had no beauty or majesty to attract us to Him, nothing in His appearance that we should desire Him," Isaiah 53:2.

Death by crucifixion was due to suffocation as the victims struggled to breathe. For Jesus, the unimaginable pain was only part of His suffering, as He also "bore our sins in His body on the tree," 1 Peter 2:24.

25–27 The group at the cross is significant; they were all women, except for John, "The disciple whom He loved." No other disciples are recorded as being present. John, who had shown no fear in the High priest's courtyard, was there, and Jesus, while on the cross, looked out for His mother by placing her in John's care.

The other gospels tell of the darkness that descended on the scene from noon to 3.00 p.m. The darkness of hell now surrounded Jesus, until His final moments. Paul reminds us that those who reject God will live in the darkness of their own minds, Romans. 1:21.

Jesus Gave Up His Spirit

28–30 At 3.00 p.m., Jesus, knowing "that all was now completed," called out, "I am thirsty." A sponge filled from a jar of wine vinegar—a cheap wine probably for the soldiers' use—was offered to Him and He drank it.

Then Jesus uttered His final words on the cross, "It is finished." These were not words of despair, but of victory. Although the final battle is still future, the victory over Satan, sin, and death was assured at that moment. As if in confirmation, "The earth shook and the rocks split." Then many "holy people" who had died came out of the tombs and appeared to many people, Matthew 27:51–53.

Even more significant, at the moment of His death, "The curtain of the temple was torn in two from the top to the bottom." The way into the holiest place where God dwelt, was open to all who would come, Matthew 27:51.

Jesus "gave up His spirit." This is in accord with His earlier declaration He would lay down His life of His own accord and then would take it up again by the authority given Him by the Father, 10:17–18. So Jesus, at the moment of his death, could look forward to His resurrection from the dead.

His death was at Passover, before Passover Friday was finished. This despite the Jew's plan that Jesus would not be killed during the feast, "or there may be a riot among the people," Matthew 26:5. But His death at Passover was God's deliberate plan, as Jesus identified Himself with the Passover lamb of Exodus 12.

At that time, each household painted the blood of a lamb on the doorframes of their houses, assuring the Israelites the angel of death, who killed the firstborn in every Egyptian household, would spare their firstborn: "When I see the blood I will pass over you," Exodus 12:13.

Those who believe in Jesus Christ, and His atoning death on Calvary's cross, and who figuratively paint His blood on the doorframes of their lives will receive the righteousness of Jesus Christ and be released from their bondage to sin and death.

Jesus was Dead

31–33   The day of Jesus' death was the day of preparation for the Sabbath next day. But falling on Passover, it was a special Sabbath. Bodies left on the cross would desecrate the Sabbath, as they were cursed by God, Deuteronomy 21:22–23.

Thus, the Jews requested that the legs of the victims be broken to ensure their death. Crucifixion caused death by asphyxiation, being hung from the wrists reduced the ability to breathe. The nails were inserted below the wrist, not through the palms, as the hand ligaments would not hold the weight of the body.

The legs were bent sideways, and one nail secured both feet through a space adjacent to the heel bones. The victim could rest his buttocks briefly on a block of wood placed halfway up the cross to enable him to breathe. He would soon slip off and the agonizing pull up from the arms and push up from the feet would repeatedly extend life and suffering.

Thus, breaking the legs would hasten death. Even after six hours, the two thieves were still alive, so the soldiers broke their legs, probably with a heavy mallet, and asphyxiation would soon follow. But Jesus was already dead. Experienced soldiers knew He was dead, and His legs were not broken. Thus was fulfilled the requirement that the bones of the Passover lamb would not be broken, Exodus 12:46 and Numbers 9:12.

34–37   One soldier pierced Jesus' side with a spear, possibly to pierce the heart as a further proof of death. Blood from the heart, together with liquid from the pericardium around the heart, issued forth. John brings to mind Zechariah 12:10, "I will pour out on the house of David and the inhabitants of Jerusalem a spirit of grace and supplication. They will look on me, the One they have pierced, and they will mourn for Him as one mourns for an only child, and grieve bitterly for Him as one grieves for a firstborn son."

Jesus, fully God and fully Man, began the fulfillment of this prophecy at the cross as the Jews gazed on their Lord. It continued as Peter preached to the Jews on the Day of Pentecost, "'Let all Israel be assured of this: God has made this Jesus, whom you crucified, both Lord and Christ.' When the people heard this, they were cut to the heart and said to Peter and the other apostles, 'Brothers, what shall we do?'" Acts 2:36–37.

Complete fulfillment will come as Christ winds up history. "Look, He is coming with the clouds, and every eye will see Him, even those who pierced Him; and all the peoples of the earth will mourn because of Him," Revelation 1:7. Compare Matthew 24:30, "At that time the sign of the Son of Man will appear in the sky, and all the nations of the earth will mourn. They will see the Son of Man coming on the clouds of the sky, with power and great glory."

Isaiah also prophesied, "But He was pierced for our transgressions," Isaiah 53:5. Those who have believed in Jesus Christ and His atoning work on Calvary will rejoice at His coming.

As far as we know, John was the only disciple to stay and watch Jesus die. He was emphatic about his witness and that his testimony is true. John also gave his reason for recording his eyewitness account, "so that you also may believe."

Jesus was Buried

38-42   Joseph of Arimathea was rich and he owned the garden tomb, Matthew 27:57 and 60. He was also a member of the Sanhedrin, who had not agreed to Jesus' death, Luke 23:50–51. Joseph needed Pilate's permission to take the body. Pilate would need to be sure Jesus was dead before releasing the body. A live body could be revived and create trouble later.

Nicodemus was also a believer in Jesus and stood up for Him, 7:51. He assisted Joseph, bringing the spices necessary for burial. Only three hours were left to take care of the body before the Sabbath began. Joseph's tomb nearby was an obvious place to lay the body before sundown. A stone was rolled over the tomb entrance, and some women noted where Jesus was laid, Matthew 27:60–61.

20

The Resurrection of Jesus

These are written that you may believe that Jesus is the Christ, the Son of God, and that by believing you may have life in His name.

John 20:31

This chapter focuses on the resurrection of Jesus Christ from the dead. It is the most momentous event of history, and critical to the Christian faith—no resurrection, no salvation. As Paul declares, "if Christ has not been raised, your faith is futile; you are still in your sins. Then those also who have fallen asleep in Christ are lost. If only for this life we have hope in Christ, we are to be pitied more than all men," 1 Corinthians 15:17–19.

That is also why John attests vigorously to the death of Jesus, to which he was an eyewitness. "The man who saw it has given testimony, and his testimony is true. He knows that he tells the truth, and he testifies so that you also may believe," 19:35–36. He repeatedly affirms Jesus alive afterward, indicating the need for belief in the risen Lord, 20:30–31, 21:24.

Note the differences between the raising of Lazarus and the resurrection of Jesus Christ. The raising of Lazarus was a temporary release from death; he would die again, but it was a powerful indicator of the new life to come. Lazarus had to be released from the grave clothes. Jesus rose from the grave clothes; they could no more hold Him than death itself could. Jesus had power over death in both cases, but in Jesus' resurrection, Jesus had authority over His own death, 10:17–18.

The Empty Tomb

1–9　　Mary Magdalene was the first to find the empty tomb, although the other gospel writers indicate she was not alone, Matthew 28:1, Mark 16:1, and Luke 24:10. Mary's use of "we" in verse 2, corroborates this. John probably wished to tell Mary Magdalene's story, as she was the first to see the risen Christ, and confirmed His resurrection, so he omitted reference to the other women. Mary also alerted Peter and John who ran to the grave to find out what had happened.

John arrived first and looked in, but Peter, on arriving, went straight in and John followed. John is careful to describe the state of the burial clothes as they found them. Their neat arrangement suggested that Jesus had risen from and through them. They were not scattered about as if Jesus had unwound them, or as grave robbers would have left them.

John "saw and believed." We are not told what he believed, although the most likely answer is that somehow Jesus had risen to life again; how or why was probably not clear to him yet. John records Jesus' resurrection was prophesied in the Old Testament, but the disciples had yet to discover this. They did not expect the resurrection.

Jesus Appears to Mary Magdalene

10–18　　After Peter and John had returned home, Mary remained weeping, and looked into the tomb. Two angels, seated at the head and feet of where Jesus' body had lain, asked why she was crying. She replied she needed to find out where the body had been taken, as she indicated in verse 2.

Turning, she saw Jesus but did not recognize Him. It seems Jesus, in His resurrected body could withhold recognition if

He so desired. Compare the two on the road to Emmaus, Luke 24:15-16. Again, Mary enquired where the body might be.

As Jesus uttered her name, "Mary," she recognized Him—His sheep recognize His voice, 10:3-4. The text suggests she tried to embrace Him. But He indicated it was not necessary to cling to Him, as He would be around for a while yet: "I have not yet returned to the Father." She and the other believers would learn of a new relationship in the Holy Spirit after He ascended, Galatians 2:20.

Jesus instructed Mary to tell the other disciples He would return "to my Father and your Father, to my God and your God." God is Father to both Jesus and believers, but in different senses. Jesus is part of the Trinity; humans become part of God's family. Mary returned to the disciples with the first news that Jesus had risen and she had actually seen Him.

Jesus Appears to the Disciples

19-20   That evening, Jesus appeared to the disciples. Despite Jesus' promise four days earlier, they had locked themselves in, fearful the Jews could still arrest them for consorting with Jesus. Jesus simply appeared in the room, suggesting He could place Himself wherever He wished to be in His risen body.

He calmed their possible fears by saying, "peace be with you," a common greeting Jesus used twice more to the disciples, verses 21 and 26. But despite His unorthodox method of appearing, He still had a physical body. He invited the disciples to see His scars in His hands and side. Luke reminds us He could eat, Luke 24:11-13. John recalls this experience in seeing and touching Jesus in his first letter, 1 John 1:1.

21-23   Jesus' work was complete. He would soon return to the Father. In these verses, Jesus commissioned the disciples to carry on His work. It was a message of peace, not from fear or trouble, but peace with God, Romans 5:1-2. To empower their work, Jesus, committed them to the Holy Spirit who would later come upon them, Acts 2:4.

His permission for the disciples' ability to forgive sins was based on their message of sins forgiven for those who believed the message of redemption. When believers share the Gospel, they have God's authority to declare forgiveness to all who repent and believe.

Jesus Appears to Thomas

24–28   Poor Thomas gets bad press most of the time, but he represents us all at some point in our pilgrimage. But Thomas particularly represents those of a skeptical mind, requiring evidence before they believe. However, they become the most fervent believers when finally convinced.

Missing on the first Sunday evening, Thomas refused to believe the fantastic tale he heard from the other disciples. If he was to believe, he wanted physical proof, to see and feel the nail and spear marks. A week later, Thomas, still protesting his unbelief, was with the disciples when Jesus appeared to the disciples again, undeterred by locked doors.

Thomas' response was unequivocal on seeing the evidence, "My Lord and my God." The full truth of the meaning of the resurrection was immediately clear to him. Standing before him was the God he professed, who had come in the flesh to give His life freely to redeem him. Based on the unfathomable sacrifice God made to redeem all, unbelief is inexcusable, 3:18 and 6:28–29.

29–31   But Jesus pointed out that although Thomas had seen and so believed, many–including us–would believe without the physical proof Thomas sought. That belief is called faith, belief in Jesus Christ, through the Word we have been given and the convicting work of the Holy Spirit.

Again, John is anxious for us to realize he records these things that we "may believe that Jesus is the Christ, the Son of God, and that by believing [we] may have life in His name." All who place their faith in the redemptive work of Jesus, God's Son, crucified for us, and His resurrection, receive this new life. They are no longer condemned, but receive peace with God.

21

Jesus Encourages His Disciples

Jesus said to them, "Come and have breakfast."
None of the disciples dared ask Him, "Who are you?" They
knew it was the Lord.

John 21:12

John features Jesus' third appearance to seven disciples in this chapter. He does not record other appearances although the other gospels do, and Paul indicates He appeared once to at least 500 at one time, 1 Corinthians 15:6. In this appearance, Jesus shows His concern for both the disciples' physical and spiritual welfare, and the future persecution they would suffer.

The Miraculous Catch of Fish

1-6   It seems likely the disciples were at a loose end. Jesus had risen, commissioned them, told them He would see them in Galilee, but they were still waiting. So what was next? Fishing seemed a reasonable alternative, yet short of the commission Jesus had given them. They spent the night fishing on the sea of Tiberius, that is the Sea of Galilee, and caught nothing.

Jesus did not criticize their fishing, in fact He improved it. They had toiled all night without any catch, and Jesus called out to them to cast their nets on the other side of the boat.

The result was dramatic: they could not haul the many fish into the boat. Although they had seen Jesus on at least two previous occasions, they still did not recognize Him.

7–10   Without any necessary recognition, John perceived it was the Lord. Who else had the power of nature at His bidding? He had stilled the storm on the sea previously, now He had provided a large catch of fish.

   Peter's reaction to John's words was immediate, jumping in the water to gain access to the shore and his Lord faster. The others followed in the boat. Jesus already had bread and fish and a fire going and invited the disciples to bring some of their fish to cook on it.

11–14   Peter, probably with help, dragged the net ashore, and even with the heavy catch, the net was not broken. Nets often broke while fishing and frequently required mending. Note the parallel story in Luke 5:4–7. Then the other disciples also recognized Jesus, not from His appearance but from the miracle of the catch.

   In this chapter to now, Jesus clearly demonstrated His concern for the everyday things of life. Sharing a meal together was as important to Him as it is to us. But His care goes beyond simply being with us. It may also include miracles that pave our way on earth whether they are apparent to us or not.

Peter is Reinstated

15–17   This long, repeated exchange between Jesus and Peter raised the question of Peter's denial—at least in Peter's mind—and whether it would bar him from the King's service. Jesus asked the question, "Do you love me?" three times; perhaps recalling Peter denied Him three times. But the question underscored the basis for service. It was not Peter's success or failure, but his love for Jesus that would constrain Peter to serve Him.

His first question included the phrase, "more than these." That could mean the life of fishing he knew before Jesus called him. Alternatively, it could mean Peter's love for the other disciples, some he had known for much of his life. A third option was whether Peter loved Jesus more than the other disciples loved Him. We don't know for sure, but each could be a hindrance to ministry. There are always distractions to draw us away from our core motivation.

The answer to Peter's protest that He loved Jesus, was met each time with caring for Jesus' lambs or sheep. Peter's love for Jesus would be revealed in his service to Jesus' other followers who would come after him. The picture for us is clear; we reveal our love for the Lord by our practical love for others.

Jesus' questions to Peter were not to assure Jesus, for as Peter said, "Lord you know all things." Clearly, they were meant to clarify Peter's thinking. Jesus reinforced Peter's reinstatement by assuring him that his love for Jesus was not measured by his past failure but on his future service to Jesus' followers.

18-19 As if in confirmation of Peter's future faithfulness, Jesus warned Peter that he would die as a martyr for Jesus. In a critical truth, meant for Peter, but a reminder we will always face potential persecution, even martyrdom, Jesus said:

> I tell you the truth, when you were younger you dressed yourself and went where you wanted; but when you are old you will stretch out your hands, and someone else will dress you and lead you where you do not want to go.

"Stretch out your hands," signified crucifixion, and tradition indicates Peter was crucified upside down. But Jesus' simple command was still "follow me," just as He had called His disciples three years before.

20-23 These verses are firstly a warning that each of us is responsible for ourselves. Peter, curious about John's fate, asked Jesus about him. Jesus affirmed that whatever fate John had in store it was not Peter's business. Peter was responsible for himself, and was not to fret over others.

A second warning here is to listen carefully to Jesus' words. Jesus' declared that even if John remained alive until He returned, it was no business of Peter's. He did not say John *would* be alive until He returned, only *if* he did. But that was construed to mean he wouldn't die, so John himself refuted that idea.

24–25   In these last two verses, John makes a last declaration for the truth. He was an eyewitness to the events he recorded in his gospel: the miracles of Jesus, His death and resurrection John describes are a true record. Jesus is the truth, John proclaims. Life can only be found in the truth, all other claims of truth are false and lead to darkness and death. Recall John's earlier assertion: "These are written that you may believe that Jesus is the Christ, the Son of God, and that by believing you may have life in His name," 20:30.

John ends his gospel by testifying to all the events he recorded as if in a court of law. John admits that he has been selective in what he wrote down. Even though John suggests earthly libraries could not contain His whole story, what he recorded is all we need to know to find life in Jesus Christ.

APPENDICIES

.

Appendix A:

The "I Am" Sayings of Jesus

1. Using the Emphatic Pronoun
    I am He: 4:26; 8:24, 28; 13:19; 18:5, 8
    I am the bread of life: 6:35, 41, 48
    I am the living bread: 6:51
    I am from Him/above   7:29; 8:23
    Cannot come where I am: 7:34, 36
    I am the light of the world: 8:12
    I am One who testifies: 8:18
    I am not from the world: 8:23; 17:14, 16
    I am: 8:58
    I am the gate: 10:7, 9
    I am the good shepherd: 10:11, 14
    I am the resurrection and the life: 11:25
    Where I am: 12:26; 17:24
    Can come where I am: 14:3; 17:24
    I am the way, the truth, the life: 14:6
    I am the (true) vine: 15:1, 5

2.   Other "I Am" sayings, without the Emphatic Pronoun

Where I am from:	7:28 (2)
I am with you:	7:33
I am not alone:	8:16; 16:32
I am the light of the world	9:5
I am in the world:	9:5; 17:13
I am God's Son:	10:36
For that (Teacher, Lord) is what I am:	13:13
I am in the Father:	14:10, 11
I am in you:	17:21
I am a king:	18:37

Note: In the English translation of John, there are many examples of "I am" used as a compound with another verb. These are not true I am sayings; for example, "I am going away," is a substitute for "I go away," or "I will go away," 8:21.

Appendix B:

Significance of the "Son of Man"

We may consider that where the New Testament names Jesus as the Son of God it refers to His deity, and similarly, Son of Man speaks of His humanity. While Jesus took on human form, His specific title as Son of Man has much greater significance. The phrase "Son of Man" had specific meaning for the Jews of Jesus' time based on Daniel 7:13-14. In these two verses we see a "Son of Man" approaching the "Ancient of Days"–the Father Himself–and specifically "coming with the clouds of heaven." John uses this phrase in Revelation because it is an identifying symbol of the Messiah expected by the Jews, and by all Christians.

The Father gave to the "One like a Son of Man" in the Daniel passage "authority, glory and sovereign power; all peoples, nations and men of every language worshiped Him. His dominion is an everlasting dominion that will not pass away, and His Kingdom is one that will never be destroyed," verses 13-14. As the Bible's definition of God is the One who may be worshiped, Exodus 20:2-4, the deity of the Son of Man is confirmed as the One all "nations and men" will worship.

Further, a study of Revelation affirms the Lamb of God, Jesus, as having the same authority and dominion. Especially in Revelation 5:6, the Lamb occupies the centre of the Throne, the same place God occupies. Jesus Himself used the phrase Son of Man to refer to Himself over eighty times in the gospels, and thirty times in John alone. His use of this title was deliberate knowing the understanding the Jews would place on it.

Two events are critical to His affirmation of His claim to be the Messiah, especially as He attached the phrase, "with the clouds," to clearly identify Himself. He used this phrase during His trial when demanded by the high priest, "Tell us if you are the Christ, the Son of God." Jesus' reply was unequivocal: "'Yes, it is as you say,' Jesus replied. 'But I say to all of you: In the future you will see the Son of Man sitting at the right hand of the Mighty One and coming *on the clouds of heaven*,'" Matthew 26:63–64 (my emphasis).

The response was dramatic. Because he did not believe Jesus, the high priest assumed Jesus' words were blasphemy and the Jews pronounced Him worthy of death. Jesus' own truthful proclamation of His identity were the words used to justify His crucifixion.

Jesus also used the full expression of His title again as He announced the circumstances of His return to earth. "At that time the sign of the Son of Man will appear in the sky, and all the nations of the earth will mourn. They will see the Son of Man coming *on the clouds of the sky*, with power and great glory," Matthew 24:30 (my emphasis).

In addition to Jesus' own remarks, read the report of Jesus' ascension into heaven, specifically, that Jesus was taken up into the clouds. Note the angel's response: "[Jesus] will come back in the same way you have seen Him go into heaven," Acts 1:9–11. He will come "with the clouds."

John also used the phrase in Revelation 1:7: "Look, He is coming with the clouds, and every eye will see Him," 1:7, as he proclaimed the glorious return of Jesus Christ.

Appendix C:

Miracles Considered as Signs

John is sparse with his recording of Jesus' miracles, using those he describes as "signs" of Christ's identity. John's recorded miracles are listed below with a brief explanation of their significance.

Water turned into wine at Cana   2:1–11
Revealed Jesus' divine power over the natural processes of the world.

Official's son healed at Capernaum   4:46–54
Showed Jesus' divine power to heal at a distance.

Sick man healed at the pool of Bethesda   5:1–9
Not only demonstrated Jesus' power to heal, but that He was also Lord of the Sabbath.

Feeding of the Five thousand   6:5–13
Revealed Jesus' power of creation.

Jesus walks on the water   6:19–21
Together with Jesus' power to still the storm, showed His power over the natural elements.

Raising Lazarus from the dead   11:1–44
Revealed Jesus' divine power over death.

The amazing catch of fish   21:1–11

Showed Jesus' power to care for the everyday needs of humankind.

Appendix D

"I Tell You the Truth"

Jesus used the saying "I tell you the truth" to emphasize critical truths He wanted His hearers to assimilate. Those found in John are listed below with a brief explanation of their importance, either to individuals or to groups. Recognize that all these sayings are relevant to Christ's followers at all times. They are universal truths.

I tell you the truth, you shall see heaven open, and the angels of God ascending and descending on the Son of Man, 1:51.

Nathanael recognized Jesus as the "Son of God" and "King of Israel." Jesus wanted to assure him and those listening, by referencing Jacob's ladder, He would fulfill His promises in response to their faith.

I tell you the truth, no one can see the Kingdom of God unless he is born again, 3:3.

Regeneration by the Holy Spirit in response to belief in God's Son is essential for entry into the Kingdom of God.

I tell you the truth, no one can enter the Kingdom of God unless he is born of water and the Spirit. 3:5.

Jesus provided an explanation of the spiritual nature of rebirth.

I tell you the truth, we speak of what we know, and we testify to what we have seen, but still you people do not accept our testimony, 3:11.

Jesus, come from the Father, spoke from His knowledge of the truth. Rejection of Jesus is rejection of the truth leading to a worldview of untrue assumptions.

"I tell you the truth, the Son can do nothing by Himself; He can do only what He sees His Father doing, because whatever the Father does the Son also does, 5:19.

Jesus claimed total identification of action and purpose with the Father.

I tell you the truth, whoever hears my word and believes Him who sent me has eternal life and will not be condemned; he has crossed over from death to life, 5:24

Jesus gives assurance that belief in Him and His message secures eternal life.

I tell you the truth, a time is coming and has now come when the dead will hear the voice of the Son of God and those who hear will live, 5:25.

Jesus will call His people from the grave to life in Him.

I tell you the truth, you are looking for me, not because you saw miraculous signs but because you ate the loaves and had your fill, 6:26.

Many follow Jesus Christ for the benefits He bestows and not for the message He brings.

I tell you the truth, it is not Moses who has given you the bread from heaven, but it is my Father who gives you the true bread from heaven. For the bread of God is He who comes down from heaven and gives life to the world, 6:32-33.

God, not Moses, provided the manna in the wilderness, and God will provide the true bread from heaven that gives eternal life.

154

I tell you the truth, he who believes has everlasting life, 6:47.
Simple faith, not high intellect, or diligent works. gains eternal life.

I tell you the truth, unless you eat the flesh of the Son of Man and drink His blood, you have no life in you, 6:53.
Jesus gives a forward look to the body and blood of Jesus given to cleanse sin and provide eternal life.

I tell you the truth, everyone who sins is a slave to sin, 8:34-35.
To seek after or acquiesce in sin results in slavery to it.

I tell you the truth, if anyone keeps my word, he will never see death, 8:51.
Acceptance of the whole message of Jesus Christ brings eternal life.

I tell you the truth . . . before Abraham was born, I am! 8:58.
Jesus asserted His existence before Abraham.

I tell you the truth, the man who does not enter the sheep pen by the gate, but climbs in by some other way, is a thief and a robber, 10:1.
Those who claim to provide a message of life apart from Jesus Christ are self-serving.

I tell you the truth, I am the gate for the sheep, 10:7.
Jesus is the only entry into God's sheepfold, that is, His family and Kingdom.

I tell you the truth, unless a kernel of wheat falls to the ground and dies, it remains only a single seed. But if it dies, it produces many seeds, 12:24.
Jesus' death is necessary to provide a multitude of others gaining new life.

155

I tell you the truth, no servant is greater than his master, nor is a messenger greater than the one who sent him, 13:16.

A servant or follower will emulate his Master's work.

I tell you the truth, whoever accepts anyone I send accepts me; and whoever accepts me accepts the one who sent me," 13:20.

To accept Jesus Christ is to recognize those He sends, Jesus Himself, and to accept the Father who sent Him.

I tell you the truth, one of you is going to betray me, 13:21.

A warning to the disciples that no group is free of traitors.

I tell you the truth, before the rooster crows, you will disown me three times! 13:38.

A warning to Peter that protestations of faithfulness are fallible.

I tell you the truth, anyone who has faith in me will do what I have been doing. He will do even greater things than these, because I am going to the Father, 14:12,

The effect of faith in Jesus' followers would exceed what Jesus was able to do during His earthly life.

I tell you the truth: it is for your good that I am going away. Unless I go away, the Counselor will not come to you, 16:7.

The work of the Holy Spirit would be broader and last longer than Jesus' influence during His earthly life.

I tell you the truth, you will weep and mourn while the world rejoices. You will grieve, but your grief will turn to joy, 16:20.

The world may exult in its achievement, often at the expense of Jesus' disciples, but their sorrow would only be temporary.

I tell you the truth, when you were younger you dressed yourself and went where you wanted; but when you are old you will stretch out your hands, and someone else will dress you and lead you where you do not want to go," 21:18.

A further warning to Peter and us that faithfulness to Jesus would lead to persecution.

Appendix E:

The Reliability of the Gospels

Introduction

There are two critical factors to the Christian faith:

1. Resurrection is essential, 1 Corinthians 15:17-19. Not just Jesus' resurrection, but ours also!

2. The Bible is the only record we have. Can we believe it? If not, our faith is still in vain.

Thus the reliability of the Bible record, especially the Gospels, is necessary and based on two approaches:

1. Criticism of the historical record.

2. Criticism on the basis of reasonableness.

Investigation must reflect the evidence we have. Some accept the record in general, but reject some detail as unreasonable. To pick and choose is to bring prejudices to bear which skew the evidence. Compare the Jesus Seminar: scriptural truth based on democratic vote leaving only a tentative "truth," always subject to revision by further vote. No certainty of our faith!

This accords with postmodern theory that truth is relative— temporary, fluid, irrelevant. Truth is obtained by what works, pragmatism, or what appears right, intuition.

"There is a way that seems right to a man, but in the end it leads to death," Proverbs 14:12, 16:25, compare Isaiah 55:8-9.

To have the security of a fixed, unalterable truth depends on belief in an omnipotent God. If there is no God, there is no organizing basis for truth, thus no truth, and no fixed reality—only passing shadows; no foundation for life, only shifting sands; no security, the ship of truth turns out to be a floating log.

Therefore, life has no ultimate meaning. It becomes superficial, temporary, including relationships, justice, security. There is no future: only the present—live for today!

"The fool says in his heart, 'There is no God,'" Psalms 14:1, 53:1. God is truth. All visions, hallucinations, dreams, personal or corporate philosophies of life, all claimed truth will stand or fall by the truth God created. Jesus said: "*I am* the Truth!" If Jesus is the truth, then the record that we have, particularly inspired writings, will stand up to legitimate critical investigation.

The Gospels are a fixed historical truth to be affirmed. The facts cannot be altered, but could be in doubt. Can we trust the Gospel writers? Like any court case, all we have are eyewitness accounts that cannot be re-enacted.

Tests for the Credibility of Witnesses

1. Honesty of Character and Motive

a) Were the writers sincere in their beliefs or evil men fabricating a message? There is no evidence that these were anything but generally good men. Their lives and teaching, and the admission of their failures attest to generally honest character. Could evil men, conspirators make up these records, particularly the sublime character of Jesus? Matthew 7:16-18, 12:33-35.

b) If the reports were fabricated, why? What reward would be gained? Every organization, Jews, all religions, Roman government, was a potential enemy to the writer's message, for God was their final authority. Their only reward was persecution and/or death—for a lie! The suicide bomber sincerely believes his actions are right and paradise is his reward. The disciples were also on a suicide mission: they were martyred for their faith!

2. Ability to Observe and Recall; to Relate without Bias

a) Matthew, Mark and John were eyewitnesses. Mark and Luke also received eyewitness accounts, Luke 1:1-4. Matthew and Luke were professionals, able to discriminate and analyze. John—an ignorant fisherman?—wrote in Greek, not Aramaic.

b) Were the writers biased? The writings do not display characteristics of fanatical writing: rant, vilification against opposition, adulation for adherents, bitterness or resentment. Rather, quiet candor and simple dignity characterize the reports. Writers record their own blunders and foibles—declarations against their own interest! Men are not likely to invent anecdotes to their own discredit.

3.   Numbers and Consistency of witnesses

a) There were least five, possibly ten appearances and up to 500 witnesses, "most of whom are still living" 1 Corinthians 15:6.

b) Detractors of the Gospels point to "discrepancies." These are mostly omissions, common to eyewitnesses that don't know or report all the facts. Reliability of corroborating witnesses is based on substantial agreement and detail variation. Total agreement suggests collusion and fraud.

Shouldn't "inspired" writings agree? Recognition of inspiration came later. Writers wrote their own accounts (Luke 1:1-4) on the prompting of the Holy Spirit.

4. Conformity with Experience

Most critics would accept the general record, but not the miraculous. Miracles not in accord with experience cannot be verified, because by their very nature miracles cannot be repeated for scientific study. However, miracles are not foreign to human experience: life itself is a miracle not yet disproved even by evolution! See C. S. Lewis, *Miracles*

5.   Coincidence of Testimony with Collateral Circumstances

Necessary when witnesses are no longer available–dead, absent or insane! Fabricated evidence is guarded by fear of detail, with hesitating, restrained, uneven, and unnatural testimony.

Honest witnesses are open, and submit numerous details. Their reporting is even, natural and unrestrained with no attempt to conceal, patch up, or reconcile. Gospel writers include without reservation manners, customs, habits and historic facts which are open to corroboration. Gospels contain many "throw away" lines that demonstrate authenticity.

None of these facts are proof in themselves. But the sum adds up to convincing circumstantial evidence of the reliability of the Gospel writers and hence the accuracy of their reporting. However, remember that corroborating evidence of our beliefs will support our faith; it does not supplant it.

Authenticity: Is John the Author?

Compare "disciple that Jesus loved," 13:23, 19:26, 20:2, 21:7, 20, 24, and claims of eyewitness, 19:35, 21:24. Early contemporaries of John claimed him as author, Irenaeus, Eusebius and Clement of Alexandria.

Is our current translation an accurate reproduction of the original? The New Testament manuscripts consist of about 5,300 Greek, 10,000 Latin, and other languages make up the rest. No other ancient writings have anywhere near the confirmation of accurate manuscript evidence. If skepticism towards the NT was directed to other ancient documents, we could be certain of very little historical data concerning the major part of the world's history!

J. B. Phillips, first modern translator of the New Testament gives his experience in his book *Ring of Truth*. He said the gospels gripped him with a clear truth, which the false gospels failed to provide. He felt like an electrician working on live circuits, the truth had that impact.

Appendix F:

Jesus' Teaching on His First Advent

Jesus taught His disciples Old Testament Scriptures concerning Himself in Luke 24:25-27, 44-49. Although those conversations were not recorded at the time, but we can find it in the disciples' writings throughout the New Testament.

The chart below lists those places where New Testament writings confirm the fulfillment of Old Testament prophecies. The first column lists the events, column two gives the New Testament reference, and the last column provides the original prophecy from the Old Testament. We use common abbreviations for Bible books in this chart. They are listed below in the order they appear.

Is. = Isaiah,
Mic. = Micah,
Hos. = Hosea,
Jer. = Jeremiah,
Ps. = Psalm,
Zech. = Zechariah,
Exod. = Exodus,
Num. = Numbers,
Deut. = Deuteronomy,
Gen. = Genesis,
Pet. = Peter.

Matthew's list of fulfilled prophecy

Much of this is repeated in Mark, Luke and John.

Born to a virgin	1:23	Is. 7:14
Born in Bethlehem	2:6	Mic. 5:2
Called from Egypt	2:15	Hos. 11:1
Killing of the children	2:18	Jer. 31:15
John the Baptist	3:3, 11:10	Is. 40:3, Mal. 3:1
Preach to the Gentiles	4:14–16	Is. 9:1-2
He would be a Healer	8:17	Is. 53:4
He would be a Servant	12:17-21	Is.42:1-4
Jews would not hear	13:13-15	Is. 6:9-10
He spoke in parables	13:35	Ps. 78:2
Hypocrisy of the Jews	15:8-9	Is. 29:13
His ride on Palm Sunday	21:4-5	Zech. 9:9, Jer. 7:11
	21:9	Ps. 118:26-27
Cleansing the Temple	21:12	Is. 56:7
Praise from the children	21:16	Ps. 8:2
Rejection of Jesus	21:42	Ps. 118:22-23
Scattering the disciples	26:31	Zech. 13:7
The potter's field	27:9	Zech. 11:12-13
Cast lots for Jesus' cloak	27:35	Ps. 22:12–18
Christ "forsaken"	27:46	Ps. 22:1

Luke's additional references

Commissioned	4:17-21	Is. 6:1-2
Died with transgressors	22:37	Is. 53:12

John's additional references

Rejection of Jesus	12:38	Is. 53:1,6
His betrayal	13:18	Ps. 41:9
Hated without reason	15:25	Ps. 69:4, 35:19
Jesus the Passover Lamb	19:36	Exod. 12:46, Num. 9:12
They see Him pierced	19:37	Zech. 12:10

Peter's references in Acts

Jesus' resurrection	2:25-28	Ps. 16:8-11
Jesus' exaltation	2:34-35	Ps. 110:1
Moses' prophecy	3.22	Deut. 18:15-19
Promise to Abraham	3.25	Gen. 12:3, 18:18, 22:18
(also to Isaac)		Gen. 26:4
(also to Jacob)		Gen. 28:14
Rejection of Jesus	4:11	Ps. 118:22

Peter's Letters

He is the Cornerstone	1 Pet. 2:6	Is. 28:16
Rejection of Jesus	1 Pet. 2:7	Ps. 118:22
He is a Rock of Offence	1 Pet. 2:8	Is. 8:14
Jesus' innocence	1 Pet. 2:22	Is. 53:9

74981511R00097

Made in the USA
Columbia, SC
10 August 2017